LISTEN

Greetings, goodbyes
& introductions ....
Background..................................
Making conversation....................
Feelings 6
Getting around.................... 7
Accommodation................... 7
Shopping............................ 7

Self-catering 10
Ordering food & drink 10
In the bar 11
Medical needs 11

CHAT   13

Meeting & greeting.................... 13
Essentials............................... 13
Breaking the language barrier 15
Personal details....................... 16
Occupations & study 17

Age 18
Feelings 18
Beliefs 19
Weather............................ 19

EXPLORE   20

Doing the sights 20
Gallery & museum hopping 21
Getting in.............................. 22

Tours............................... 22
Top 5 day trips from Paris 24
Top 10 Paris sights 25

SHOP   27

Essentials............................... 27
Paying................................... 28
Clothes & shoes....................... 29

Hot Paris shop spots............ 29
Books & music.................... 30
Photography 31

ENJOY   32

What's on? 32
Meeting up 33

Small talk 33

EAT & DRINK 34

Choosing & booking 34
Eateries 35
Ordering 36
Nonalcoholic drinks 36
Alcoholic drinks........................... 37
In the bar 37

Buying food 38
Special diets & allergies 39
On the menu 40
Menu decoder 41
Top eats on the go 48

SERVICES 49

Post office 49
Bank... 49
Phone 50

Mobile/cell phone...................... 51
Internet...................................... 52

GO 53

Directions................................... 53
Getting around........................... 54
Tickets & luggage 55

Bus, metro, taxi & train 57
Car & motorbike hire 59
Road signs.................................. 60

SLEEP 61

Finding accommodation 61
Booking ahead & checking in 62

Requests & queries...................... 63
Checking out 65

WORK 66

Introductions 66
Business needs............................ 67

After the deal 67

HELP 68

Emergencies 68
Police 69

Health 70
Symptoms, conditions & allergies 71

LOOK UP 74

Numbers 74
Colours 74
Times & dates 75

English–French dictionary 77
French–English dictionary 93

LISTEN

Welcome to *Listen* – the quickest way to chat like a local. This chapter will guide you through each of the 99 essential phrases listed on your Fast Talk Audio CD – just check inside the back cover! Plug in those headphones and follow along with the track listing below.

Greetings, goodbyes & introductions
track

1	Hello.	*Bonjour.*
2	Goodbye.	*Au revoir.*
3	How are you?	*Comment allez-vous?* pol
		Ça va? inf
4	Fine thanks, and you?	*Bien, merci. Et vous?* pol
		Bien, merci. Et toi? inf
5	My name is ...	*Je m'appelle ...*
6	Pleased to meet you.	*Enchanté(e).* m/f
7	This is my partner.	*Voici mon partenaire.*

Background
track

8	Where are you from?	*Vous venez d'où?* pol
9	I'm from ...	*Je viens de ...*
10	I'm married.	*Je suis marié(e).* m/f
11	I'm single.	*Je suis célibataire.* m&f
12	What's your phone number?	
	Quel est votre numero de téléphone? pol	
	Quel est ton numero de téléphone? inf	

5

13   What's your email address?   *Quel est votre e-mail?* pol
                                           Quel est ton e-mail? inf

Making conversation

track

14   What's your occupation?   *Vous faites quoi comme métier?* pol
                                           Tu fais quoi comme métier? inf

15   I'm an office worker.   *Je suis un employé de bureau.* m

16   I'm a manual worker.   *Je suis ouvrier.* m
                                           Je suis une ouvrière. f

17   I'm a businessperson.   *Je suis un homme d'affaires.* m
                                           Je suis une femme d'affaires. f

18   I'm a student.   *Je suis un étudiant.* m

19   I'm an artist.   *Je suis un artiste.* m

20   How old are you?   *Quel âge avez-vous?* pol
                                           Quel âge as-tu? inf

21   I'm (25) years old.   *J'ai (vingt-cinq) ans.*

22   Do you like art?   *Aimes-tu l'art?*

23   Do you like sport?   *Aimes-tu le sport?*

24   Do you like reading?   *Aimes-tu lire?*

25   Do you like to dance?   *Aimes-tu danser?*

26   Do you like travelling?   *Aimes-tu voyager?*

Feelings

track

27   I'm hungry.   *J'ai faim.*

28   I'm cold.   *J'ai froid.*

29   I'm hot.   *J'ai chaud.*

30   I'm thirsty.   *J'ai soif.*

31   Are you okay?   *Est-tu bien?*

Getting around

track

32	Is this the bus (to Paris)?	*Est-ce le bus (pour Paris)?*
33	Is this the plane (to Paris)?	*Est-ce l'avion (pour Paris)?*
34	Is this the train (to Paris)?	*Est-ce le train (pour Paris)?*
35	How much Is It to …?	*C'est combien pour aller à …?*
36	Is this taxi available?	*Vous êtes libre?*
37	What time does it leave?	*À quelle heure est-ce qu'il part?*
38	Where's the city centre?	*Où est-ce qu'il y a le centre-ville?*
39	Where's a hotel?	*Où est-ce qu'il y a l'hôtel?*
40	Where's a market?	*Où est-ce qu'il y a le marché?*

Accommodation

track

41	Where's a camping ground?
	Où est-ce qu'on peut trouver un terrain de camping?
42	Can you recommend somewhere cheap?
	Est-ce que vous pouvez recommander un logement pas cher?
43	Can you recommend somewhere good?
	Est-ce que vous pouvez recommander un bon logement?
44	How much is it per night?
	Quel est le prix par nuit?
45	I'd like to book a room, please.
	Je voudrais réserver une chambre, s'il vous plaît.

Shopping

track

46	Where's the supermarket?	*Où est le supermarché?*
47	Where's a bank?	*Où est la banque?*

48 Where can I buy ...?
    Où puis-je acheter ...?
49 Can I look at it?
    Est-ce que je peux le voir?
50 What's your lowest price?
    Quel est votre meilleur prix?
51 Can you write down the price?
    Pouvez-vous écrire le prix?
52 I'd like a receipt, please.
    Je voudrais un reçu, s'il vous plaît.

Photography

track

53 I need a (200) speed film for this camera.
    J'ai besoin d'un pellicule rapidité (deux cent) pour cet appareil.
54 I need an APS film for this camera.
    J'ai besoin d'un pellicule APS pour cet appareil.
55 I need a black and white film for this camera.
    J'ai besoin d'un pellicule en noir et blanc pour cet appareil.
56 Can you load my film?
    Pouvez-vous charger ma pellicule?
57 Can you develop this film?
    Pouvez-vous développer cette pellicule?
58 When will it be ready?
    Quand est-ce que cela sera prêt?

Going out

track

59 I feel like going to the movies.
    Je voudrais aller au cinéma.
60 I feel like going to the theatre.
    Je voudrais aller au théâtre.

61   **I feel like going to a concert.**
Je voudrais aller à un concert.

62   **Where can I find clubs?**
Où sont les clubs?

63   **Where can I find gay venues?**
Où sont les boîtes gaies?

64   **Where can I find pubs?**
Où sont les pubs?

Sightseeing
track

65   **When's the next day trip?**
C'est quand la prochaine excursion d'une journée?

66   **How long is the tour?**
L'excursion dure combien de temps?

67   **Is the admission charge included?**
Est-ce que l'admission est incluse?

68   **What time should we be back?**
On doit rentrer pour quelle heure?

Finding a place to eat/drink
track

69   **Can you recommend a restaurant?**
Est-ce que vous pouvez me conseiller un restaurant?

70   **Can you recommend a café?**
Est-ce que vous pouvez me conseiller un café?

71   **Do you have vegetarian food?**
Vous faites les plats végétariens?

72   **Is there a vegetarian restaurant near here?**
Y a-t-il un restaurant végétarien par ici?

73   **I'd like a table for (five) please.**
Je voudrais une table pour (cinq) personnes, s'il vous plaît.

9

74　I'd like the nonsmoking section.
　　Je voudrais un endroit pour non-fumeurs.

75　Can you recommend a bar?
　　Est-ce que vous pouvez me conseiller un bar?

Self-catering

track

76　How much is (a kilo)?
　　Combien (le kilo)?

77　I'd like (200) grams.
　　Je voudrais (deux cent) grammes.

78　I'd like (six) slices.
　　Je voudrais (six) tranches.

79　What's the local speciality?
　　Quelle est la spécialité locale?

Ordering food & drink

track

80　I'd like to see the drinks list, please.
　　Je voudrais la carte des boissons, s'il vous plaît.

81　I'd like the menu, please.
　　Je voudrais la carte, s'il vous plaît.

82　What would you recommend?
　　Qu'est-ce que vous conseillez?

83　A cup of coffee (with milk).
　　Un café (au lait).

84　A cup of tea (with milk).
　　Un thé (au lait).

85　I'd like the bill, please.
　　Je voudrais l'addition, s'il vous plaît.

In the bar

track

86	What would you like?	*Qu'est-ce que vous voulez?*
87	I'll buy you a drink.	*Je vous offre un verre.*
88	A glass of beer.	*Un verre de bière.*
89	A glass of white wine.	*Un verre de vin blanc.*
90	A glass of red wine.	*Un verre de vin rouge.*
91	Champagne.	*Champagne.*
92	Cheers!	*Santé!*

Medical needs

track

93 **Help!**
Au secours!

94 **I need a doctor who speaks English.**
J'ai besoin d'un médecin qui parle anglais.

95 **Could I see a female doctor?**
Est-ce que je peux voir une femme médecin?

96 **I've run out of my medication.**
Je n'ai plus de médicaments.

97 **Where's the nearest dentist?**
Où y a t-il un dentiste par ici?

98 **Where's the nearest hospital?**
Où y a t-il un hôpital par ici?

99 **Where's a night pharmacy?**
Où y a t-il une pharmacie de nuit par ici?

LISTEN

Language name: French

French is known to its native speakers as *le français*, ler fron·say.

Language family: Romance

French belongs to the Romance family of languages and is a close relative of both Italian and Spanish. It's also quite closely related to English.

Key country & secondary countries:

France is the key French-speaking country but almost 30 countries cite French as an official language, among them Belgium, Luxembourg, Switzerland and the province of Quebec, Canada. France's colonial expansion spread French to countries in Africa, the Pacific and the Caribbean.

Approximate number of speakers:

80 million people speak French as their first language. A further 50 million speak it as their second language.

Donations to English:

Due to an invasion of England in the 11th century, French has contributed widely to the vocabulary of English, so you're sure to recognise many words.

Grammar:

The structure of French holds no major surprises for English speakers as the two languages are quite closely related.

Pronunciation:

The sounds of French can almost all be found in English. The few sounds that do differ from English, including the silent *h* and the throaty *r* will be familiar to most through their contact with French via film and television.

Abbreviations used in this book:

m	masculine	sg	singular	pol	polite
f	feminine	pl	plural	inf	informal

CHAT
Meeting & greeting

Hello.	*Bonjour.*	bon·zhoor
Hi.	*Salut.*	sa·lew
Good morning/ afternoon.	*Bonjour.*	bon·zhoor
Good evening/night.	*Bonsoir.*	bon·swar
See you later.	*À bientôt.*	a byun·to
Goodbye.	*Au revoir.*	o rer·vwar
Mr/Sir	*Monsieur (M)*	mer·syer
Ms/Mrs	*Madame (Mme)*	ma·dam
Miss	*Mademoiselle (Mlle)*	mad·mwa·zel
Doctor	*Docteur (Dr)*	dok·ter

How are you?

Comment allez-vous? pol		ko·mon ta·lay·voo
Ça va? inf		sa va

Essentials

Yes.	*Oui.*	wee
No.	*Non.*	non
Please.	*S'il vous plaît.*	seel voo play
Thank you (very much).	*Merci (beaucoup).*	mair·see (bo·koo)
You're welcome.	*Je vous en prie.*	zher voo zon·pree
Excuse me.	*Excusez-moi.*	ek·skew·zay·mwa
Sorry.	*Pardon.*	par·don

13

Fine. And you?
Bien, merci. — byun mair·see
Et vous/toi? pol/inf — ay voo/twa

What's your name?
Comment vous appelez-vous? pol — ko·mon voo za·play·voo
Comment tu t'appelles? inf — ko·mon tew ta·pel

My name is …
Je m'appelle … — zher ma·pel …

I'd like to introduce you to …
Je vous présente … — zher voo pray·zont …

I'm pleased to meet you.
Enchanté(e). m/f — on·shon·tay

It's been great meeting you.
Ravi d'avoir fait — ra·vee da·vwar fay
votre/ta connaissance. pol/inf — vo·trer/ta ko·nay·sons

This is my …	*Voici mon/ma …* m/f	vwa·see mon/ma …
child	*enfant* m&f	on·fon
colleague	*collègue* m&f	ko·leg
friend	*ami(e)* m/f	a·mee
husband	*mari* m	ma·ree
partner (intimate)	*partenaire* m&f	par·ter·nair
wife	*femme* f	fam

I'm here …	*Je suis ici …*	zher swee zee·see …
for a holiday	*pour les vacances*	poor lay va·kons
on business	*pour le travail*	poor ler tra·vai
to study	*pour les études*	poor lay zay·tewd
with my family	*avec ma famille*	a·vek ma fa·mee·yer
with my partner	*avec mon/ma*	a·vek mon/ma
	partenaire m/f	par·ter·nair

How long are you here for?

Vous êtes ici pour	voo·zet ee·see poor
combien de temps? pol	kom·byun der tom
Tu es ici pour	tew ay zee·see poor
combien de temps? inf	kom·byun der tom

I'm here for ... days/weeks.

Je reste ici ...	zher rest ee·see ...
jours/semaines.	zhoor/ser·men

For numbers, see the box feature in **LOOK UP**, page 74.

Here's my ...	*Voici mon ...*	vwa·see mon ...
What's your ...?	*Quel est votre ...?* pol	kel ay vo·trer ...
	Quel est ton ...? inf	kel ay ton ...
address	*adresse*	a·dress
email address	*e-mail*	ay mel
fax number	*numéro de fax*	new·may·ro der faks
home number	*numéro de téléphone*	new·may·ro der tay·lay·fon
mobile number	*numéro de portable*	new·may·ro der por·ta·bler
work number	*numéro au travail*	new·may·ro tra·vai

Breaking the language barrier

Do you speak English?

Parlez-vous anglais?	par·lay·voo ong·glay

Does anyone speak English?

Y a-t-il quelqu'un qui parle anglais?	ee·a·teel kel·kung kee par long·glay

Do you understand?	*Comprenez-vous?*	kom·prer·nay·voo
I understand.	*Je comprends.*	zher kom·pron
I don't understand.	*Je ne comprends pas.*	zher ner kom·pron pa
I speak a little.	*Je parle un peu.*	zher parl um per
What does '*ça va*' mean?	*Que veut dire 'ça va'?*	ker ver deer sa va

How do you …?	*Comment …?*	ko·mon …
pronounce this	*le prononcez-vous*	ler pro·non·say voo
write '*bonjour*'	*est-ce qu'on écrit*	es kon ay·kree
	'bonjour'	bon·zhoor

Could you	*Pourriez-vous …,*	poo·ree·yay voo …
please …?	*s'il vous plaît?*	seel voo play
repeat that	*répéter*	ray·pay·tay
speak more	*parler plus*	par·lay plew
slowly	*lentement*	lon·ter·mon
write it down	*l'écrire*	lay·kreer

Personal details

I'm from …	*Je viens …*	zher vyun …
England	*de l'Angleterre*	der long·gler·tair
Ireland	*de l'Irlande*	der leer·lond
Scotland	*de l'Ecosse*	der lay·kos
the USA	*des États Unis*	day zay·taz ew·nee

Where are you from?

Vous venez d'où? pol		voo ver·nay doo
Tu viens d'où? inf		tew vyun doo

I'm ...	*Je suis ...*	zher swee ...
single	*célibataire*	say·lee·ba·tair
married	*marié(e)* m/f	mar·yay
separated	*séparé(e)* m/f	say·pa·ray
divorced	*divorcé(e)* m/f	dee·vor·say

Occupations & study

I'm a ...	*Je suis un/une ...* m/f	zher sweez un/ewn ...
businessperson	*homme/femme d'affaires* m/f	om/fem da·fair
chef	*cuisinier/ cuisinière* m/f	kwee·zee·nyay/ kwee·zee·nyair
teacher	*professeur* m&f	pro·fay·ser

I work in ...	*Je travaille dans ...*	zher tra·vai don ...
education	*l'enseignement*	lon·sen·yer·mon
health	*la santé*	la son·tay
sales & marketing	*la vente et le marketing*	la vont ay ler mar·kay·teeng

I'm studying ...	*Je fais des études ...*	zher fay day zay·tewd ...
engineering	*d'ingénieur*	dun·zhay·nyer
French	*de français*	der fron·say
media	*des médias*	day may·dya

For other occupations, see the dictionary in **LOOK UP**, page 77.

Age

How old are you? (to an adult)		
Quel âge avez-vous?		kel azh a·vay·voo
How old are you? (to a child)		
Quel âge as-tu?		kel azh a·tew
How old is your son/daughter?		
Quel âge a votre fils/fille?		kel azh a vo·trer fees/fee·yer
I'm ... years old.		
J'ai ... ans.		zhay ... on
He/She is ... years old.		
Il/Elle a ... ans.		eel/el a ... on

For your age, see the numbers box in **LOOK UP**, page 74.

Feelings

I'm ...	*J'ai ...*	zhay ...
I'm not ...	*Je n'ai pas ...*	zher nay pa ...
Are you ...?	*Avez-vous ...?* pol	a·vay voo ...
	As-tu ...? inf	a·tew ...
cold	*froid*	frwa
hungry	*faim*	fum
thirsty	*soif*	swaf
I'm ...	*Je suis ...*	zher swee ...
I'm not ...	*Je ne suis pas ...*	zher ner swee pa ...
Are you ...?	*Êtes-vous ...?* pol	et voo ...
	Es-tu ...? inf	ay·tew ...
happy	*content(e)* m/f	kon·ton(t)
sad	*triste*	treest
satisfied	*satisfait(e)* m/f	sa·tees·fay(t)

Beliefs

I'm ...	*Je suis ...*	zher swee ...
I'm not ...	*Je ne suis pas ...*	zher ner swee pa ...
agnostic	*agnostique*	ag·no·steek
atheist	*athée*	a·tay
Buddhist	*bouddhiste*	boo·deest
Catholic	*catholique*	ka·to·leek
Christian	*chrétien(ne)* m/f	kray·tyun/kray·tyen
Hindu	*hindou(e)* m/f	un·doo
Jewish	*juif/juive* m/f	zhweef/zhweev
Muslim	*musulman(e)* m/f	mew·zewl·mon/
		mew·zewl·man
practising	*pratiquant(e)* m/f	pra·tee·kon(t)
Protestant	*protestant(e)* m/f	pro·tay·ston(t)

Weather

What's the weather like?
Quel temps fait-il? kel tom fay·teel

(Today) It's ...	*(Aujourd'hui)*	(o·zhoor·dwee)
	Il fait ...	eel fay ...
Will it be ...	*Est-ce qu'il fera*	es·keel fe·ra
tomorrow?	*... demain?*	... der·mun
(very) cold	*(très) froid*	(tray) frwa
(very) hot	*(très) chaud*	(tray) sho

It's cloudy.	*Le temps est couvert.*	ler tom ay koo·vair
It's raining.	*Il pleut.*	eel pler
It's sunny.	*Il fait beau.*	eel fay bo
It's snowing.	*Il neige.*	eel nezh

19

EXPLORE
Doing the sights

What would you do if you had just one day?
Que feriez-vous si vous n'aviez ker fe·ryay voo see voo nav·yay
qu'un jour de disponible? kun zhoor der dees·pon·ee·bler

Do you have information on local places of interest?
Avez-vous des renseignements a·vay·voo day ron·sen·yer·mon
sur les endroits à visiter? sewr lay zon·drwa a vee·zee·tay

I'd like to see ...
J'aimerais voir ... zhem·ray vwar ...

I have (one day).
J'ai (un jour). zhay (un zhoor)

What's that?
Qu'est-ce que c'est? kes·ker say

Who made it?
Qui l'a fait? kee la fay

How old is it?
Ça date de quand? sa dat der kon

I'd like a/an ...	*Je voudrais ...*	zher voo·dray ...
audio set	*un écouteur*	un ay·koo·ter
catalogue	*un catalogue*	ung ka·ta·log
city map	*un plan de la ville*	um plon der la veel
guide	*un guide*	ung geed
guidebook	*un guide*	ung geed
(in English)	*(en anglais)*	(on ong·lay)
local map	*une carte*	ewn kart
	de la région	der la ray·zhyon

Could you take a photograph of me?
Pouvez-vous me prendre   poo·vay·voo mer pron·drer
en photo?   on fo·to

Can I take photographs?
Je peux prendre des photos?   zher per pron·drer day fo·to

I'll send you the photograph.
Je vous enverrai la photo.   zher voo zon·vay·ray la fo·to

Gallery & museum hopping

When's the ...	... *ouvre à*	... oo·vrer a
open?	*quelle heure?*	kel er
gallery	*La galerie*	la gal·ree
museum	*le musée*	ler mew·zay

What's in the collection?
Qu'est-ce qu'il y a   kes·keel·ya
dans la collection?   don la ko·lek·syon

It's an exhibition of ...
C'est une exposition de ...   set ewn ek·spo·zee·syon der ...

I like the works of ...
J'aime l'œuvre de ...   zhem ler·vrer der ...

It reminds me of ...
Cela me rappelle ...   ser·la mer ra·pel ...

... art	*l'art ...,*	lar ...
contemporary	*contemporain*	kon·tom·po·run
impressionist	*impressionniste*	um·pray·syo·neest
modernist	*moderniste*	mo·dair·neest
Renaissance	*de la Renaissance*	der la rer·nay·sons

Getting in

What's the admission charge?
Quel est le prix d'admission?   kel ay ler pree dad·mee·syon

It costs (seven euros).
Ça coûte (sept euros).   sa koot (set er·ro)

What time does it ...?	Quelle est l'heure ...?	kel ay ler ...
close	de fermeture	der fer·mer·tewr
open	d'ouverture	doo·vair·tewr

Is there a discount for ...?	Il y a une réduction pour les ...?	eel ya ewn ray·dewk·syon poor lay ...
children	enfants	zon·fon
families	familles	fa·mee·yer
groups	groupes	groop
pensioners	personnes du troisième âge	pair·son dew trwa·zyem azh
students	étudiants	zay·tew·dyon

Tours

Can you recommend a ...?	Pouvez-vous me recommander une ...?	poo·vay·voo mer rer·ko·mon·day ewn ...
boat trip	excursion en bateau	eks·kewr·syon en ba·to
day trip	excursion d'une journée	eks·koor·syon dewn zhoor·nay
tour	excursion	eks·kewr·syon

22

When's the next ...?	C'est quand la prochaine ...?	say kon la pro·shen ...
boat trip	excursion en bateau	eks·kewr·syon en ba·to
day trip	excursion d'une journée	eks·koor·syon dewn zhoor·nay
tour	excursion	eks·koor·syon

Is ... included?	Est-ce que .., est inclus(e)? m/f	es·ker ... ay tung·klew(z)
accommodation	le logement m	ler lozh·mon
the admission charge	le prix m d'entrée	ler pree don·tray
food	la nourriture f	la noo·ree·tewr
transport	le transport m	ler trons·por

EXPLORE appears as side tab

Do I need to take ...?
Dois-je prendre ...? dwa·zher pron·drer ...

The guide will pay.
Le guide va payer. ler geed va pay·yay

The guide has paid.
Le guide a payé. ler geed a pay·yay

How long is the tour?
L'excursion dure combien de temps? leks·kewr·syon dewr kom·byun der tom

What time should we be back?
On doit rentrer pour quelle heure? on dwa ron·tray poor kel er

I'm with them.
Je suis avec eux. zher swee za·vek er

I've lost my group.
J'ai perdu mon groupe. zhay pair·dew mon groop

Have you seen a group of (Australians)?
Avez-vous vu un groupe (d'Australiens)? a·vay voo vew un groop (dos·tra·lyun)

23

Top 5 day trips from Paris

If the pace of Paris becomes overwhelming, join the Parisians in escaping to some of these out-of-town oases:

Château de Fontainebleau   sha·to der fon·ten·blo
Surrounded by beautiful gardens, the Château de Fontainebleau is one of the most charmingly decorated and furnished châteaux in France. Strolling in the adjacent woods is a favourite Parisian pastime.

Cathédrale de Chartres   ka·tay·dral der shar·trer
A magnificent medieval cathedral renowned for its Gothic and Romanesque spires, ornamental portals and awe-inspiring stained-glass windows.

Disneyland Paris   dees·nay·lond pa·ree
The most popular fee-paying attraction in Europe, it comprises an amusement park, Disney Studios and Disneyland village, featuring restaurants, bars and even a skating rink.

Musée de Claude Monet   mew·say der clod mo·nay
à Giverny   a zhee·ver·nee
The home of impressionist Claude Monet from 1883–1926 in the delightful village of Giverny. The gardens surrounding the house provided the inspiration for some of Monet's most famous paintings, including the *Water Lilies* series.

Versailles   ver·sai
The site of the grandest and most famous château in France, Versailles was the kingdom's political capital and the seat of the royal court for more than a century, until the Revolution in 1789. The château is also famous for its splendid ornamental gardens and fountains.

EXPLORE

Top 10 Paris sights

It would take a lifetime to unearth all the riches that Paris has to offer. If you don't have that much time on your hands, make sure you pack in a few of these famous highlights:

Arc de Triomphe
ark der tree·omf

Commissioned by Napoleon, the Arc de Triomphe towers 50m above Place Charles de Gaulle, the vast traffic roundabout from which 12 boulevards, including the Champs Élysées, radiate.

Centre Pompidou
son·trer pom·pee·doo

The Pompidou Centre has amazed and delighted visitors since it was built in the mid-1970s — not just for its outstanding collection of modern art, but for its radical, colourful 'inside out' architectural statement.

Cimetière du Père Lachaise
seem·tyer dew pair la·shayz

Père Lachaise is the most visited necropolis in the world. Many famous people are buried here, including the composer Chopin, singer Edith Piaf, rock star Jim Morrison, dancer Isadora Duncan, the writers Molière, Oscar Wilde and Marcel Proust, and the artists Delacroix and Modigliani.

Jardin du Luxembourg
zhar·dun dew look·som·boor

This 25-hectare park with its Franco-Italian style terraces, floral displays and chestnut groves is a favourite Parisian fair-weather playground. Children can enjoy the boating pond, puppet theatre, pony rides and carousel.

Montmartre
mon·mar·trer

Montmartre is crowned by the wedding-cake-like church Basilique du Sacré Cœur, one of Paris' most recognisable landmarks. Despite the throngs of tourists, Montmartre retains a bohemian village feel with its narrow twisting cobblestone streets, buskers and street artists.

Musée d'Orsay
mew·zay dor·say

Once a train station, the *Musée d'Orsay* now houses under its vault a superb collection of French Impressionist and Post-Impressionist works. On display are France's national collection of paintings, sculptures, *objets d'art* and other works, including those by Rodin, Renoir and Van Gogh.

Musée du Louvre
mew·zay dew loo·vrer

The Louvre is arguably the world's greatest art museum but despite its overwhelming richness many would-be visitors are daunted by its sheer size. An enjoyable way to sample its great works is to buy a map-guide to direct you to the works you really want to see.

Musée Rodin
mew·zay ro·dun

One of the most tranquil spots in the city, this is also many visitors' favourite Paris museum. A huge body of the vital sculptor's works are housed inside his magnificent 18th-century residence and in the surrounding rose garden.

Notre Dame
no·trer dam

The cathedral of Notre Dame, built between 1163 and 1345, is a masterpiece of French Gothic architecture. It has also been Catholic Paris' ceremonial focus for seven centuries. The building is remarkable for its sublime balance, and its immense interior is a marvel of medieval engineering.

Tour Eiffel
toor e·fel

Named for its designer Gustave Eiffel, this icon of mass tourism reaches a height of 320m. Even the most jaded visitor will feel a frisson of excitement as they ascend through the girders, and the panoramic views from any of the three levels are breathtaking. At night, transformed by clever illumination, it floats as though built of nothing more substantial than filaments of light.

SHOP
Essentials

Where's ...?	*Où est-ce qu'il y a ...?*	oo es·keel ya ...
a bank	*une banque*	ewn bongk
a cake shop	*une pâtisserie*	ewn pa·tees·ree
a grocery store	*une épicerie*	ewn ay·pee·sree

Where can I buy ...?
Où puis-je acheter ...? oo pweezh ash·tay ...

I'd like to buy ...
Je voudrais acheter ... zher voo·dray ash·tay ...

Do you have any others?
Vous en avez d'autres? voo zon a·vay dô·trer

Can I look at it?
Est-ce que je peux le/la voir? m/f es·ker zher per ler/la vwar

I'm just looking.
Je regarde. zher rer·gard

Could I have it wrapped?
Pouvez-vous l'envelopper? poo·vay·voo lon·vlo·pay

Could I have a bag, please?
Puis-je avoir un sac, s'il vous plaît? pweezh a·vwar un sak seel voo play

Does it have a guarantee?
Est-ce qu'il y a une garantie? es keel ya ewn ga·ron·tee

Can I have it sent overseas?
Pouvez-vous me poo·vay·voo mer
l'envoyer à l'étranger? lon·vwa·yay a lay·tron·zhay

Can I pick it up later?
Je peux passer le/la zher per pa·say ler/la
prendre plus tard? m/f pron·drer plew tar

It's faulty/broken.
C'est défectueux/cassé. say·day·fek·twer/ka·say

I'd like ..., please. *Je voudrais ...,* zher voo·dray ...
  s'il vous plaît. seel voo play

  a discount *un rabais* un ra·bay
  my money back *un remboursement* un rom·boors·mon
  to change this *échanger ceci* ay·shonzh·ay ser·see
  to return this *rapporter ceci* ra·por·tay ser·see

Paying

How much is it?
Ça fait combien? sa fay kom·byun

Can you write down the price?
Pourriez-vous écrire le prix? poo·ryay·voo ay·kreer ler pree

Can I have smaller notes?
Pourriez-vous me donner des poo·ryay voo mer do·nay day
petites coupures? per·teet koo·pewr

Do you accept ...? *Est-ce que je* es·ker zher
  peux payer avec ...? per pay·yay a·vek ...
  credit cards *une carte* ewn kart
  de crédit der kray·dee
  debit cards *une carte* ewn kart
  de débit der day·bee
  travellers *des chèques* day shek
  cheques *de voyages* der vwa·yazh

I'd like ... *Je voudrais ...* zher voo·dray ...
  a receipt *un reçu* un rer·sew
  my change *ma monnaie* ma mo·nay

That's too expensive.
C'est trop cher.   say tro shair

Do you have something cheaper?
Avez-vous quelque   a·vay·voo kel·ker
chose de moins cher?   shoz der mwun shair

Clothes & shoes

I'm looking for ...	*Je cherche ...*	zher shairsh ...
shoes	*un jean*	un zheen
shoes	*des chaussures*	day sho·sewr
underwear	*des sous-vêtements*	day soo·vet·mon

Can I try it on?
Puis-je l'essayer?   pwee·zher lay·say·yay

Hot Paris shop spots

Paris is the home of chic and a sublime place to shop. Avid consumers and window-shoppers alike can sate their appetites at the following locales:

Abbesses (18e) – vintage clothing • streetwear • fabrics • music
Marais (3e) – hip boutiques • books • music • homewares • quirky speciality stores
Opéra (9e) – major department stores • clothing • perfume • cosmetics
Place Vendôme (1er) – jewellery • luxury goods
Quartier Latin (5e) – books • stationery
Rue de Paradis (10e) – glass • crystal • china • Limoges wear
Rue de Rivoli & Les Halles (1er & 2e) – international brands • clothes • shoes • books • music • toys • perfume
St-Germain (6e) – designer clothes & accessories • shoes • antiques • speciality stores

My size is (42).
Je fais du (quarante-deux). zher fay dew (ka·ront·der)

Do you have this in size (36)?
*Vous avez la même
chose en taille (trente-six)?* voo za·vay la mem
shoz on tai (tront·sees)

It doesn't fit.
Ce n'est pas la bonne taille. ser nay pa la bon tai

small	*petit*	per·tee
medium	*moyen*	mwai·un
large	*large*	larzh

Books & music

Is there an English-language bookshop?
*Y a-t-il une librairie de
langue anglaise?* ya·teel ewn lee·brair·ee der
long ong·glayz

Is there an English-language section?
Y a-t-il un rayon anglais? ya·teel un ray·yon ong·glay

Do you have a/an	*Avez-vous . . .*	a·vay·voo . . .
... in English?	*en anglais?*	on ong·glay
novel by ...	*un roman de . . .*	un ro·mon der . . .
entertainment guide	*un guide des spectacles*	ung geed day spek·ta·kler
I'd like a ...	*Je voudrais . . .*	zher voo·dray . . .
map (city)	*un plan de la ville*	um plon der la veel
map (road)	*une carte routière*	ewn kart roo·tyair
newspaper (in English)	*un journal (en anglais)*	un zhoor·nal (on ong·glay)
pen	*un stylo*	un stee·lo
postcard	*une carte postale*	ewn kart pos·tal

I'd like (a) ...	Je voudrais ...	zher voo·dray ...
blank CD	un CD vierge	un say·day vyerzh
CD	un CD	un say·day
headphones	un casque	ung kask

I'm looking for a CD by ...
Je cherche un CD de ... zher shairsh un say·day der ...

What's his/her best recording?
Quel est son meilleur kel ay som may·yer
enregistrement? on·rer·zhees·trer·mon

Can I listen to it here?
Je peux l'écouter ici? zher per lay·koo·tay ee·see

Photography

I need ...	J'ai besoin d'une	zhay ber·zwun dewn
film for this	pellicule ... pour	pay·lee·kewl ... poor
camera.	cet appareil.	say ta·pa·ray
APS	APS	a·pay·es
B&W	en noir et blanc	on nwar ay blong
colour	couleur	koo·ler
(100) ASA	(cent) ASA	(son) a es a

Can you ...?	Pouvez-vous ...?	poo·vay·voo ...
develop	développer	day·vlo·pay
this film	cette pellicule	set pay·lee·kewl
load my	charger ma	shar·zhay ma
film	pellicule	pay·lee·kewl

How much is it to develop this film?
C'est combien pour say kom·byun poor
développer cette pellicule? day·vlo·pay set pay·lee·kewl

When will it be ready?
Quand est-ce que cela sera prêt? kon tes·ker ser·la ser·ra pray

SHOP

ENJOY
What's on?

What's on …?	Qu'est-ce qu'on joue …?	kes-kon zhoo …
locally	dans le coin	don ler kwun
this weekend	ce week-end	ser week-end
today	aujourd'hui	o-zhoor-dwee
tonight	ce soir	ser swar

Where are the …?	Où sont les …?	oo son lay …
clubs	clubs	klerb
discos	discothèques	dees-ko-tek
gay hangouts	boîtes gaies	bwat gay
places to eat	restaurants	res-to-ron
pubs	pubs	perb

Is there a local … guide?	Y a-t-il un programme …?	ya-teel un pro-gram …
entertainment	des spectacles	day spek-ta-kler
film	des films	day feelm

I'd like to go to a/the …	Je voudrais aller …	zher voo-dray a-lay …
ballet	au ballet	o ba-lay
bar	au bar	o bar
café	au café	o ka-fay
cinema	au cinéma	o see-nay-ma
concert	à un concert	a ung kon-sair
nightclub	en boîte	on bwat
opera	à l'opéra	a lo-pay-ra
restaurant	au restaurant	o res-to-ron
theatre	au théâtre	o tay-a-trer

Meeting up

What time shall we meet?
On se retrouve à quelle heure?   on ser rer·troov a kel er

Where will we meet?
On se retrouve où?   on ser rer·troov oo

I'll pick you up at (seven).
Je viendrais te chercher   zher vyun·dray te shair·shay
à (sept heures).   a (set er)

Let's meet at …	*On peut se retrouver …*	on per ser rer·troo·vay …
(eight o'clock)	*à (huit heures)*	a (wee ter)
the (entrance)	*devant (l'entrée)*	der·von (lon·tray)

Small talk

What do you do in your spare time?
Que fais-tu pendant tes loisirs?   ker fay·tew pon·don tay lwa·zeer

Do you like …?	*Aimez-vous/*	em·ez voo/
	Aimes-tu …? pol/inf	em·tew …
I like …	*J'aime …*	zhem …
I don't like …	*Je n'aime pas …*	zher nem pa …
dancing	*danser*	don·say
going to concerts	*aller aux concerts*	a·lay o kon·sair
going to	*aller au*	a·lay o
the theatre	*théâtre*	tay·a·trer

I like …	*J'aime les …*	zhem lay…
I don't like …	*Je n'aime pas les …*	zher nem pa lay …
action movies	*films d'action*	feelm dak·syon
French films	*films français*	feelm fron·say
sci-fi films	*films de*	feelm der
	science-fiction	syons feek·syon

ENJOY

EAT & DRINK

breakfast	*petit-déjeuner* m	per·tee day·zher·nay
lunch	*déjeuner* m	day·zher·nay
dinner	*dîner* m	dee·nay
snack	*casse-croûte* m	kas·kroot

Choosing & booking

Where would you go for a celebration?
On va où pour faire la fête?   on va oo poor fair la fet

Can you recommend a ...?	*Est-ce que vous pouvez me conseiller ...?*	es·ker voo poo·vay mer kon·say·yay ...
bar	*un bar*	um bar
café	*un café*	ung ka·fay
restaurant	*un restaurant*	un res·to·ron

Where would you go for ...?	*Où est-ce qu'on trouve ...?*	oo es kon troov ...
a cheap meal	*les restaurants bon marché*	lay res·to·ron bom mar·shay
fine dining	*un bon restaurant*	un bon res·to·ron
local specialities	*les spécialités locales*	lay spay·sya·lee·tay lo·kal

I'd like ..., please.	*Je voudrais ..., s'il vous plaît.*	zher voo·dray ... seel voo play
a table for (five)	*une table pour (cinq) personnes*	ewn ta·bler poor (sungk) pair·son
smoking/ nonsmoking	*pour fumeurs/ non-fumeurs*	poor few·mer/ non·few·mer

Eateries

Sampling and savouring French cuisine is one of the great joys of a visit to France. Give free rein to your gastronomic curiosity at these establishments:

auberge   o·bairzh
serves traditional country fare In a relaxed atmosphere

bistro   bees·tro
can be anything from a pub with inexpensive snacks to a bar with a fully fledged restaurant menu

brasserie   bras·ree
serves inexpensive full meals, drinks and coffee from early in the morning to late at night

café   ka·fay
an important focal point for social life and, in addition to coffee, it sells basic food including baguette sandwiches

cafétéria   ka·fay·tay·ree·a
offers a good selection of cheap dishes you can select and pay for at a counter

crêperie   krep·ree
specialises in *crêpes* (thin pancakes) which are folded or rolled over a filling

relais routier   re·lay roo·tyay
a truck stop café — these places provide a hearty break and are not as rough and ready as the UK or US equivalent

restaurant   res·to·ron
typically specialises in a particular cuisine and is usually open only at set times for lunch and dinner

restaurant libre-service   res·to·ronlee·brer ser·vees
a self-service restaurant similar to a *cafétéria*

salon de thé   sa·lon der tay
a trendy and pricey establishment that serves sweet and savoury pastries and salads, in addition to tea and coffee

Ordering

What would you recommend?
Qu'est-ce que vous conseillez?   kes·ker voo kon·say·yay

I'd like ...,	*Je voudrais ...,*	zher voo·dray ...
please.	*s'il vous plaît.*	seel voo play
the bill	*l'addition*	la·dee·syon
the chicken	*le poulet*	ler poo·lay
the menu	*la carte*	la kart
a napkin	*une serviette*	ewn sair·vyet
pepper	*le poivre*	ler pwa·vrer
salt	*le sel*	ler sel
the set menu	*le menu du jour*	ler mer·new dew zhoor
the wine list	*la carte des vins*	la kart day vun

I'd like it ...	*J'aime ça ...*	zhem sa ...
medium	*à point*	a pwun
rare	*saignant*	say·nyon
well-done	*bien cuit*	byun kwee
with the dressing on the side	*avec la sauce à côté*	a·vek la sos a ko·tay

Nonalcoholic drinks

(cup of) coffee	*(un) café* m	(ung) ka·fay
(cup of) tea	*(un) thé* m	(un) tay
black ...	*... noir*	... nwar
... with milk	*... au lait*	... o lay
... without/ with sugar	*... sans/avec sucre*	... son/a·vek sew·krer

orange juice	*jus* m *d'orange*	zhew do·ronzh
soft drink	*boisson* f *non-alcoolisée*	bwa·son non·al·ko·lee·zay

	... water	eau f	o ...
	hot	chaude	shod
	sparkling mineral	minérale gazeuse	mee·nay·ral ga·zerz
	still mineral	minérale non-gazeuse	mee·nay·ral nong·ga·zerz

Alcoholic drinks

beer	bière f	byair
brandy	cognac m	ko·nyak
champagne	champagne m	shom·pan·yer
cocktail	cocktail m	kok·tel

a bottle of ... wine	une bouteille de vin ...	ewn boo·tay der vun ...
a glass of ... wine	un verre de vin ...	un vair der vun ...
red	rouge	roozh
sparkling	mousseux	moo·ser
white	blanc	blong

a ... of beer	... de bière	... der byair
bottle	une bouteille	ewn boo·tay
glass	un verre	un vair

| a shot of | un petit verre | um per·tee vair |
| (whisky) | de (whisky) | der (wees·kee) |

In the bar

I'll have (a gin).
Je prends (un gin). zher pron (un zheen)

Same again, please.
La même chose, s'il vous plaît. la mem shoz seel voo play

I'll buy you a drink.
Je vous offre un verre.   zher voo zo·frer un vair

What would you like?
Qu'est-ce que vous voulez?   kes·ker voo voo·lay

It's my round.
C'est ma tournée.   say ma toor·nay

Cheers!
Santé!   son·tay

Buying food

What's the local speciality?
Quelle est la   kel ay la
spécialité locale?   spay·sya·lee·tay lo·kal

What's that?
Qu'est ce que c'est?   kes ker say

How much?
Combien?   kom·byun

How much is (a kilo)?
C'est combien pour   say kom·byun poor
(un kilo)?   (un kee·lo)

I'd like ...	*Je voudrais ...*	zher voo·dray ...
(200) grams	*(deux cents) grammes*	(der son) gram
(two) kilos	*(deux) kilos*	(der) kee·lo
(three) pieces	*(trois) morceaux*	(trwa) mor·so
(six) slices	*(six) tranches*	(see) tronsh
some of that/ those	*de ça*	der sa

cooked	cuit(e) m/f	kwee(t)
dried	sec/sèche m/f	sek/sesh
fresh	frais/fraîche m/f	fray/fresh
frozen	surgelé(e) m/f	sewr·zher·lay

Enough, thanks.	Ça ira, merci.	sa ee·ra mair·see
A bit more, please.	Encore un peu, s'il vous plaît.	ong·kor un per seel voo play
Less, thanks.	Moins, s'il vous plaît.	mwun seel voo play

Special diets & allergies

Is there a (vegetarian) restaurant near here?

Y a-t-il un restaurant (Vegétarien) par ici? — ya teel un res·to·ron (vay·zhay·ta·ryun) par ee·see

Do you have (vegetarian) food?

Vous faites les repas (végétariens)? — voo fet lay rer·pa (vay·zhay·ta·ryun)

Could you prepare a meal without ...?	Pouvez-vous préparer un repas sans ...?	poo·vay·voo pray·pa·ray un rer·pa son ...
butter	du beurre	dew ber
eggs	des œufs	day zer
meat stock	du bouillon gras	dew boo·yon gra

I'm ...	Je suis ...	zher swee ...
vegan	végétalien(ne) m/f	vay·zhay·ta·lyun/ vay·zhay·ta·lyen
vegetarian	végétarien(ne) m/f	vay·zhay·ta·ryun/ vay·zhay·ta·ryen

I'm allergic to ...	Je suis allergique ...	zher swee za·lair·zheek ...
caffeine	à la caféine	a la ka·fay·een
dairy produce	aux produits laitiers	o pro·dwee lay·tyay
eggs	aux œufs	o zer
gluten	au gluten	o glew·ten
nuts	aux noix	o nwa
seafood	aux fruits de mer	o frwee der mair

I don't eat/drink ...
Je ne mange/bois pas ...　　zher ner monzh/bwa pa ...

For more on allergies, see **HELP**, page 73 and **LOOK UP**, page 77.

On the menu

Amuse-gueules	a·mewz·gerl	appetisers
Soupes	soop	soups
Entrées	on·tray	entrees
Salades	sa·lad	salads
Plats Principaux	pla prun·see·po	main courses
Desserts	day·sair	desserts
Boissons	bwa·son	drinks
Apéritifs	a·pay·ree·teef	aperitifs
Spiritueux	spee·ree·tew·er	spirits
Bières	byair	beers
Vins Mousseux	vun moo·ser	sparkling wines
Vins Blancs	vun blong	white wines
Vins Rouges	vun roozh	red wines
Vins de Dessert	vun der day·sair	dessert wines

For more help reading the menu, see the **Menu decoder**, page 41.

EAT & DRINK

Menu decoder

à la vapeur	a la va·per	steamed
abricot m	ab·ree·ko	apricot
agneau m	a·nyo	lamb
agneau m *de lait*	a·nyo de lay	baby lamb
ail m	ai	garlic
aloyau m	a·lwa·yo	sirloin
amandes f pl	a·mond	almonds
ananas m	a·na·nas	pineapple
anchois m	on·shwa	anchovies
andouille f	on·doo·yer	sausage made of intestines
aneth m	a·net	dill
anguille f	ong·gee·yer	eel
artichaut m	ar·tee·sho	artichoke
asperges f	a·spairzh	asparagus
au poivre	o pwa·vrer	with pepper sauce
aubergine f	o·bair·zheen	aubergine • eggplant
avec	a·vek	with
avocat m	a·vo·ka	avocado
banane f	ba·nan	banana
bar m	bar	bass
beignet m	be·nyay	fritter
betterave f	be·trav	beetroot
bifteck m	beef·tek	beefsteak
bisque f	beesk	shellfish soup
bœuf m	berf	beef
bœuf m *bourguignon*	berf boor·geen·yon	beef stew with onions & mushrooms in a burgundy sauce
bouillabaisse f	bwee·a·bes	fish soup from Marseille
bouilli(e) m/f	boo·yee	boiled

bouillon m	boo·yon	broth
bourride f	boo·reed	Provençal white fish soup
braisé(e) m/f	bre·se	braised
brème f	brem	bream
brochet m	bro·shay	pike
cacahuètes f pl	ka·ka·wet	peanuts
caille f	kai·yer	quail
calmar m	kal·mar	squid
canard m	ka·nar	duck
canard m *sauvage*	ka·nar so·vazh	wild duck
caneton m	kan·ton	duckling
carbonnade f	kar·bo·nad	selection of chargrilled meats
carottes f pl	ka·rot	carrots
carrelet m	ka·re·lay	plaice
cassis m	ka·sees	blackcurrant
céleri m	sayl·ree	celery
cerfeuil m	ser·fer·yee	chervil
cerises f pl	se·rees	cherries
cervelle f	ser·vel	brains
champignons m pl	shom·pee·nyon	mushrooms
châtaignes f pl	sha·tayn·nyer	chestnuts
chevreuil m	sher·vrer·yer	venison
chou m	shoo	cabbage
chou-fleur m	shoo·fler	cauliflower
choucroute f	shoo·kroot	pickled cabbage • sauerkraut
ciboulette f	see·boo·let	chives
citron m	see·tron	lemon
citrouille f	see·troo·yer	pumpkin
cochon m *de lait*	ko·shon de lay	suckling pig
concombre m	kon·kom·brer	cucumber
consommé m	kon·so·may	clear soup

contre-filet m	kon·trer fee·lay	sirloin (steak)
coq m *au vin*	kok o vun	chicken cooked with wine, onions & mushrooms
coquilles Saint-Jacques f pl	ko·kee·yer sun zhak	scallops
cornichon m	kor·nee·shon	gherkin
côtelette f	ko·te·let	cutlet
coulis m	koo·lee	purée, usually of fruit or vegetable
courgette f	koor·zhet	courgette · zucchini
crevettes f pl *grises*	kre·vet grees	shrimps
crevettes f pl *roses*	kre·vet ros	prawns
cru(e) m/f	krew	raw
crudités m pl	krew·dee·tay	raw vegetables with dressings
cuisses f pl *de grenouilles*	kwees de grer·noo·yer	frogs legs
cuit(e) m/f	kwee(t)	cooked
cuit(e) m/f *au four*	kwee(t) o foor	baked
darne f	darn	fish cutlet
datte f	dat	date
daurade f	do·rad	sea bream
dinde f	dund	turkey
dindon m	dun·don	turkey
dindonneau m	dun·do·no	young turkey
doux/douce m/f	doo/doos	mild · sweet
du jour	dew zhoor	of the day
écrevisses f pl	e·kre·vees	crayfish
émincé(e) m/f	ay·mun·say	thinly sliced
entrecôte f	on·tre·kot	ribsteak
épaule f	ay·pol	shoulder
épinards m pl	ay·pee·nar	spinach

escargots m pl	es·kar·go	snails
estouffade f	es·too·fad	stew
estragon m	es·tra·gon	tarragon
faisan m	fay·zan	pheasant
fait(e) m/f à la maison	fay(t) a la may·son	homemade
farci(e) m/f	far·see	stuffed
fenouil m	fer·noo·yer	fennel
figue f	feeg	fig
filet m	fee·lay	fillet
flamiche f	fla·meesh	leek quiche
foie m	fwa	liver
fraises f pl	frez	strawberries
framboises f pl	from·bwaz	raspberries
fromage m	fro·mazh	cheese
fricassée f	free·ka·say	stewed meat & vegetables in creamy sauce
fumé(e) m/f	few·may	smoked
gambas f pl	gam·bas	king prawns
garniture f	gar·nee·tewr	garnish
gelée f	zhe·lay	jelly
gibier m	zheeb·yay	game
gigot m	zhee·go	leg
grillade f	gree·yad	mixed grill
grillé(e) m/f	gree·yay	grilled
groseilles f pl	gro·zay·yer	gooseberries
hachis m	a·shee	hash (chopped mince meat or vegetables)
haricots m pl *verts*	a·ree·ko ver	French or string beans
homard m	o·mar	lobster
huîtres m pl	wee·trer	oysters
jambon m	zhom·bon	ham
laitance m	lay·tons	roe
laitue f	lay·tew	lettuce

langoustines f pl	long·goo·steen	scampi or Dublin Bay prawns
langue f	long	tongue
lapin m	la·pun	rabbit
lard m	lar	bacon
laurier m	lo·ryay	bay leaf
légumes m pl	lay·gewm	vegetables
lentilles f pl	lon·tee·yer	lentils
lièvre f	lye·vrer	hare
longe f	lonzh	loin
lotte f	lot	monkfish
loup m *de mer*	loo de mer	bass
maison f	may·son	of the house
mange-tout m	monzh·too	sugar peas • snowpeas
maquereau m	ma·kro	mackerel
mariné(e) m/f	ma·ree·nay	marinated
marjolaine f	mar·zho·len	marjoram
marrons m pl	ma·ron	chestnuts
menthe f	mont	mint
menu m dégustation	mer·new day·gew·sta·syon	tasting menu
merguez f	mair·gez	spicy red sausage
merlan m	mer·lon	whiting
mirabelle f	mee·ra·bel	plum
moelle f	mwal	marrow
moules f pl	mool	mussels
moules f pl marinières	mool ma·ree·nyair	mussels with shallots in white-wine sauce
moutarde f	moo·tard	mustard
mûres f pl	mewr	blackberries
noisettes f pl	nwa·zet	hazelnuts
noix f	nwa	nuts • walnuts
noix f *de coco*	nwa de ko·ko	coconut
oie f	wa	goose

oignon m	o·nyon	onion
olives f pl	o·leev	olives
orange f	o·ronzh	orange
palourdes f pl	poo·lard	clams
pamplemousse m	pom·ple·moos	grapefruit
pané(e) m/f	pa·nay	crumbed
pastèque f	pas·tek	watermelon
patate f *douce*	pa·tat doos	sweet potato
pâté m	pa·tay	paté • pie
pâtes f pl	pat	pasta
pêche f	pesh	peach
persil m	per·see	parsley
petits pois m pl	per·tee pwa	peas
piquant m	pee·kon	spicy hot
pistou m	pees·too	pesto
poché(e) m/f	po·shay	poached
poêle f	pwal	frying pan
poêlé(e) m/f	pwa·lay	pan-fried
poire f	pwar	pear
poireau m	pwa·ro	leek
pois chiches m pl	pwa sheesh	chickpeas
poisson m	pwa·son	fish
poitrine f *de porc*	pwa·treen de por	pork belly
poitrine f *de veau*	pwa·treen de vo	breast of veal
poivre m	pwa·vrer	pepper
poivron m	pwa·vron	capsicum • pepper
pomme f	pom	apple
pomme f *de terre*	pom der tair	potato
porc f	por	pork
potage m	po·tazh	thick soup, usually vegetable
potiron m	po·tee·ron	pumpkin
poularde f	poo·lard	fatted chicken
poulet m	poo·lay	chicken

poulpe m	poolp	octopus
prune f	prewn	plum
pruneau m	prew·no	prune
queue f *de bœuf*	ker de berf	oxtail
radis m	ra·dee	radish
ragoût m	ra·goo	stew of meat or poultry & vegetables
raifort m	ray·for	horseradish
raisins m pl	ray·sun	grapes
ratatouille f	ra·ta·too·yer	eggplant, zucchini, tomato & garlic dish
rillettes f pl	ree·yet	potted meat (pork or goose)
riz m	ree	rice
rognons m pl	ro·nyon	kidneys
romarin m	ro·ma·run	rosemary
rôti(e) m/f	ro·tee	roast
saint-pierre m	sun·pyair	John Dory (fish)
sanglier m	song·glee·yay	wild boar
sardines f pl	sar·deen	sardines
sauge f	sozh	sage
saumon m	so·mon	salmon
séché(e) m/f	se·shay	dried
sel m	sel	salt
selle f	sel	saddle (of meat)
steak m *frites*	stek freet	steak with chips
steak m *tartare*	stek tar·tar	raw minced beef, raw onion & egg yolk
thon m	ton	tuna
thym m	tun	thyme
topinambours m pl	to·pee·nam·boor	Jerusalem artichokes
tournedos m	toor·ne·do	thick slices of fillet
tourte f	toort	pie
tranché(e) m/f	tran·shay	sliced
tripes f pl	treep	tripe

47

truffes f pl	trewf	truffles
truite f	trweet	trout
veau m	vo	veal
venaison f	ver·nay·son	venison
vinaigre m	vee·nay·grer	vinegar
viande f	vyond	meat
volaille f	vo·lai	poultry

Top eats on the go

If you're out and about and hunger strikes unheralded, join the French in sampling some of these hasty, tasty treats:

baguette sandwich   ba·get son·dweech
crispy bread stick sliced open and filled

choucroute   shoo·kroot
sauerkraut — a variation is *choucroute garnie* sauerkraut served with assorted fresh and smoked meats and sausages

crêpes   krep
large, paper-thin pancakes served with various fillings

croque madame   krok ma·dam
grilled or pan-fried ham and cheese sandwich with a fried egg on top

croque monsieur   krok mer·syer
same as a *croque madame* but without the egg

moules et frites   mool ay freet
mussels served with chips or French fries

pain au chocolat   pun o sho·ko·la
flat croissant with chocolate filling

plat cuisiné   pla kwee·see·nay
pre-prepared meal from a *traiteur* (delicatessen)

steak frites   stek freet
minute steak with chips or French fries

SERVICES
Post office

English	French	Pronunciation
I want to send a ...	Je voudrais envoyer ...	zher voo·dray on·vwa·yay ...
fax	un fax	un faks
letter	une lettre	ewn le·trer
parcel	un colis	ung ko·lee
postcard	une carte postale	ewn kart pos·tal
I want to buy ...	Je voudrais acheter ...	zher voo·dray ash·tay ...
an envelope	une enveloppe	ewn on·vlop
stamps	des timbres	day tum·brer
Please send it (to Australia) by ...	Envoyez-le (en Australie) ..., s'il vous plaît.	on·vwa·yay·ler (on os·tra·lee) ... seel voo play
airmail	par avion	par a·vyon
express post	en exprès	on neks·pres
regular post	en courrier normal	on koor·yay nor·mal
surface mail	par voie de terre	par vwa der tair

Bank

Where's the nearest ...?	Où est ... le plus proche?	oo ay ... ler plew prosh
automatic teller machine	le guichet automatique de banque	ler gee·shay o·to·ma·teek der bongk
foreign exchange office	le bureau de change	ler bew·ro der shonzh

What time does the bank open?
À quelle heure ouvre la banque?   a kel er oo·vrer la bongk

I'd like to ...	*Je voudrais ...*	zher voo·dray ...
Where can I ...?	*Où est-ce que je peux ...?*	oo es·ker zher per ...
arrange a transfer	*faire un virement*	fair un veer·mon
cash a cheque	*encaisser un chèque*	on·kay·say un shek
change a travellers cheque	*changer des chèques de voyage*	shon·zhay day shek der vwa·yazh
change money	*changer de l'argent*	shon·zhay der lar·zhon
get a cash advance	*une avance de crédit*	ewn a·vons der kray·dee
withdraw money	*retirer de l'argent*	rer·tee·ray der lar·zhon

What's the ...?	*Quel est ...?*	kel ay ...
charge	*le tarif*	ler ta·reef
commission	*la commission*	la ko·mee·syon
exchange rate	*le taux de change*	ler to der shonzh

Phone

What's your phone number?
Quel est votre numéro de téléphone?   kel ay vo·trer new·may·ro der tay·lay·fon

Where's the nearest public phone?
Où est le téléphone public le plus proche?   oo ay ler tay·lay·fon pewb·leek ler plew prosh

I'd like to buy a phone card.
Je voudrais acheter une carte téléphonique.   zher voo·dray ash·tay ewn kart tay·lay·fo·neek

The number is ...		
Le numéro est ...		ler new·may·ro ay ...

I want to make a ...	*Je veux faire ...*	zher ver fair ...
call	*un appel*	un a·pel
	téléphonique	tay·lay·fo·neek
local call	*un appel local*	un a·pel lo·kal
reverse-charge/	*un appel*	un a·pel
collect call	*en PCV*	on pay say vay

How much does ... cost?	*Quel est le prix ...?*	kel ay ler pree ...
a (three)-minute	*d'une*	dewn
call	*communication*	ko·mew·nee·ka·syon
	de (trois) minutes	der (trwa) mee·newt
each extra	*de chaque minute*	der shak mee·newt
minute	*supplémentaire*	sew·play·mon·tair

SERVICES

Mobile/cell phone

What are the rates?
Quels sont les tarifs? kel son lay ta·reef

(30c) per (30) seconds.
(Trente cents) pour (30) secondes. (tront sent) poor (tront) sgond

I'd like a/an ...	*Je voudrais ...*	zher voo·dray ...
adaptor plug	*une prise*	ewn preez
	multiple	mewl·tee·pler
charger for	*un chargeur pour*	un shar·zher poor
my phone	*mon portable*	mom por·ta·bler
mobile/cell phone	*louer un*	loo·ay um
for hire	*portable*	por·ta·bler
prepaid mobile/	*un portable*	um por·ta·bler
cell phone	*pré-payé*	pray·pay·yay
SIM card for	*une carte SIM*	ewn kart seem
the network	*pour le réseau*	poor ler ray·zo

51

Internet

Where's the local Internet café?
*Où est le cybercafé
du coin?*
oo ay ler see·bair·ka·fay
dew kwun

How much per hour?
C'est combien l'heure?
say kom·byun ler

How much per page?
C'est combien la page?
say kom·byun la pazh

Can I burn a CD?
Je peux brûler un CD?
zher per brew·lay un say day

Can you help me change to English-language preference?
*Pouvez-vous m'aider à
choisir l'Anglais comme
langue de préférence?*
poo·vay·voo may·day a
shwa·zeer long·glay kom
longk der pray·fay·rons

It's crashed.
C'est tombé en panne.
say tom·bay om pan

I'd like to …	Je voudrais …	zher voo·dray …
check my email	consulter mon courrier électronique	kon·sewl·tay mong koor·yay ay·lek·tro·neek
get Internet access	me connecter à l'internet	mer ko·nek·tay a lun·tair·net
use a printer	utiliser une imprimante	ew·tee·lee·zay ewn um·pree·mont
use a scanner	utiliser un scanner	ew·tee·lee·zay un ska·nair

Do you have …?	Avez-vous …?	a·vay·voo …
PCs	des PCs	day pay ·say
Macs	des Macs	day mak
a zip drive	une lecteur zip	ewn lek·ter zeep

GO
Directions

Where's (the station)?
Où est (la gare)?　　　　　　oo ay (la gar)

Where's (a grocery store)?
Où est-ce qu'il y a (une épicerie)?　　oo e· skeel·ya (ewn ay·pee·sree)

I'm looking for the (Metropole Hotel).
Je cherche (L'Hôtel Métropole).　　zher shairsh (lo·tel may·tro·pol)

Can you show me (on the map)?
Pouvez-vous m'indiquer　　　poo·vay·voo mun·dee·kay
(sur la carte)?　　　　　　(sewr la kart)

What's the address?
Quelle est l'adresse?　　　　kel ay la·dres

How do I get there?
Comment faire pour y aller?　　ko·mon fair poor ee a·lay

How far is it?　　*C'est loin?*　　　　say lwun

It's ...	C'est ...	say ...
behind ...	derrière ...	dair·yair ...
beside ...	à côté de ...	a ko·tay der ...
far away	loin d'ici	lwun dee·see
here	ici	ee·see
in front of ...	devant ...	der·von ...
left	à gauche	a gosh
near here	près d'ici	pray dee·see
on the corner	au coin	o kwun
opposite ...	en face de ...	on fas der ...
right	à droite	a drwat
straight ahead	tout droit	too drwa
there	là	la

GO

It's ...	C'est à ...	say ta ...
(10) minutes	(dix) minutes	(dee) mee·newt
(100) metres	(cent) mètres	(son) me·trer

Turn ...	Tournez ...	toor·nay ...
at the corner	au coin	o kwun
at the traffic lights	aux feux	o fer
left	à gauche	a gosh
right	à droite	a drwat

by boat	en bateau	om ba·to
by bus	en bus	om bews
on foot	à pied	a pyay
by metro	en métro	on may·tro
by taxi	en taxi	on tak·see
by train	en train	on trun

north	nord	nor
south	sud	sewd
east	est	est
west	ouest	west

Getting around

What time does the ... leave?	À quelle heure part ...?	a kel er par ...
boat	le bateau	ler ba·to
bus	le bus	ler bews
ferry	le bac	ler bak
plane	l'avion	la·vyon
train	le train	ler trun
tram	le tramway	ler tram·way

GO

54

What time's	Le ... bus passe	ler ... bews pas
the ... bus?	à quelle heure?	a kel er
first	premier	prer·myay
last	dernier	dair·nyay
next	prochain	pro·shun

How many stops to ...?
Combien d'arrêts jusqu'à ? kom·byun da·ray zhews·ka ...

Is this seat taken?
Est-ce que cette place es·ker set plas
est occupée? ay o·kew·pay

That's my seat.
C'est ma place. say ma plas

Can you tell me when we get to ...?
Pouvez-vous me dire quand poo·vay·voo mer deer kon
nous arrivons à ...? noo za·ree·von a ...

I want to	Je veux	zher ver
get off ...	descendre ...	day·son·drer ...
at (Nantes)	à (Nantes)	a (nont)
here	ici	ee·see

Tickets & luggage

Where can I buy a ticket?
Où peut-on acheter un billet? oo per·ton ash·tay um bee·yay

Do I need to book?
Est-ce qu'il faut es·keel fo
réserver une place? ray·zer·vay ewn plas

How long does the trip take?
Le trajet dure ler tra·zhay dewr
combien de temps? kom·byun der tom

How much is it?	C'est combien?	say kom·byun
I'd like to ... my ticket, please.	Je voudrais ... mon billet, s'il vous plaît.	zher voo·dray ... mom bee·yay seel voo play
cancel	annuler	a·new·lay
change	changer	shon·zhay
collect	passer prendre	pa·say pron·drer
confirm	confirmer	kon·feer·may
One ... ticket (to Lyon), please.	Un billet ... (pour Lyon), s'il vous plaît.	um bee·yay ... (poor lyon) seel voo play
1st-class	de première classe	der prem·yair klas
2nd-class	de seconde classe	der sgond klas
child's	au tarif enfant	o ta·reef on·fon
one-way	simple	sum·pler
return	aller et retour	a·lay ay rer·toor
student's	au tarif étudiant	o ta·reef ay·tew·dyon
I'd like a/an ... seat.	Je voudrais une place ...	zher voo·dray ewn plas ...
aisle	côté couloir	ko·tay koo·lwar
nonsmoking	non-fumeur	non·few·mer
smoking	fumeur	few·mer
window	côté fenêtre	ko·tay fe·ne·trer

Is there air-conditioning?
Est-qu'il y a la climatisation? es·keel ya la klee·ma·tee·za·syon

Is there a toilet?
Est-qu'il y a des toilettes? es·keel ya day twa·let

Is it a direct route?
Est-ce que c'est direct? es·ker say dee·rekt

GO

56

What time do I have to check in?
Il faut se présenter à
l'enregistrement à quelle heure?
    eel fo ser pray·zon·tay a
    lon·rer·zhee·strer·mon a kel er

Can I get a stand-by ticket?
Pourrais-je avoir un
ticket stand-by?
    poo·rayzh av·war un
    tee·ke stond·bai

Where's the baggage claim?
Où est la livraison
des bagages?
    oo ay la lee·vray·zon
    day ba·gazh

I'd like a luggage locker.
Je voudrais une
consigne automatique.
    zher voo·dray ewn
    kon·see·nyer o·to·ma·teek

Can I have some coins/tokens?
Je peux avoir des
pièces/jetons?
    zher per a·vwar day
    pyes/zher·ton

My luggage	*Mes bagages*	may ba·gazh
has been ...	*ont été ...*	on tay·tay ...
damaged	*endommagés*	on·do·ma·zhay
lost	*perdus*	per·dew
stolen	*volés*	vo·lay

Bus, metro, taxi & train

Which bus goes to ...?
Quel bus va à ...?
    kel bews va a ...

Is this the bus to ...?
Est-ce que c'est le bus pour ...?
    es·ker say ler bews poor ...

What station is this?
C'est quelle gare?
    say kel gar

What's the next station?
Quelle est la prochaine gare?   kel ay la pro·shen gar

Does this train stop at (Amboise)?
Est-ce que ce train   es·ker se trun
s'arrête à (Amboise)?   sa·ret a (om·bwaz)

Do I need to change trains?
Est-ce qu'il faut changer de train?   es·keel fo shon·zhay der trun

Which carriage is for (Bordeaux)?
C'est quelle voiture pour   say kel vwa·tewr poor
(Bordeaux)?   (bor·do)

Which line goes to ...?
Quelle ligne va à ...?   kel lee·nyer va a ...

Which platform does it depart from?
Il part de quel quai?   eel par der kel kay

Which is the dining car?
Où est le wagon-restaurant?   oo ay ler va·gon·res·to·ron

Where's the taxi stand?
Où est la station de taxis?   oo ay la sta·syon der tak·see

I'd like a taxi ...	*Je voudrais un taxi ...*	zher voo·dray un tak·see ...
at (9 o'clock)	*à (neuf heures)*	a (nerf er)
now	*maintenant*	mun·ter·non
tomorrow	*demain*	der·mun

Is this taxi free?
Vous êtes libre?   voo zet lee·brer

Please put the meter on.
Mettez le compteur,   me·tay ler kon·ter
s'il vous plaît.   seel voo play

How much is it to ...?
C'est combien pour aller à ...?   say kom·byun poor a·lay a ...

Please take me to (this address).
Conduisez-moi à   kon·dwee·zay mwa a
(cette adresse), s'il vous plaît.   (set a·dres) seel voo play

Please ...	*..., s'il vous plaît.*	... seel voo play
slow down	*Roulez plus*	roo·lay plew
	lentement	lont·mon
wait here	*Attendez ici*	a·ton·day ee·see

Stop ...	*Arrêtez-vous ...*	a·ray·tay voo ...
at the corner	*au coin de la rue*	o kwun der la rew
here	*ici*	ee·see

Car & motorbike hire

I'd like to hire a ...	*Je voudrais louer ...*	zher voo·dray loo·way ...
(small/large) car	*une (petite/ grosse) voiture*	ewn (per·teet/ gros) vwa·tewr
manual	*une manuel*	ewn ma·nwel
motorbike	*une moto*	ewn mo·to

with ...	*avec ...*	a·vek ...
air-conditioning	*climatisation*	klee·ma·tee·za·syon
anti-freeze	*antigel*	on·tee·zhel
snow chains	*chaînes à neige*	shen a nezh

How much for ... hire?	*Quel est le tarif par ...?*	kel ay ler ta·reef par ...
daily	*jour*	zhoor
hourly	*heure*	er
weekly	*semaine*	ser·men

Does that include ...?	*Est-ce que ... est compris(e)?* m/f	es·ker ... ay kom·pree(z)
insurance	*l'assurance* f	la·sew·rons
mileage	*le kilométrage* m	ler kee·lo·may·trazh

What's the speed limit?
Quelle est la vitesse maximale permise?
kel ay la vee·tes mak·see·mal per·meez

Is this the road to ...?
C'est la route pour ...?
say la root poor ...

Where's a petrol station?
Où est-ce qu'il y a une station-service?
oo es·keel ya ewn sta·syon·ser·vees

(How long) Can I park here?
(Combien de temps) Est-ce que je peux stationner ici?
(kom·byun der tom) es·ker zher per sta·syo·nay ee·see

diesel	*diesel* m	dyay·zel
leaded	*au plomb*	o plom
petrol/gas	*essence* f	e·sons
regular	*ordinaire*	or·dee·nair
unleaded	*sans plomb*	son plom

Road signs

Cédez la Priorité	say·day la pree·o·ree·tay	Give Way
Entrée	on·tray	Entrance
Péage	pay·azh	Toll
Sens Interdit	sons un·ter·dee	No Entry
Sens Unique	sons ew·neek	One way
Sortie	sor·tee	Exit
Stop	stop	Stop

SLEEP
Finding accommodation

Where's a ...?	*Où est-ce qu'on peut trouver ...?*	oo es·kon per troo·vay ...
bed and breakfast	*une pension*	ewn pon·syon
camping ground	*un terrain de camping*	un tay·run der kom·peeng
guesthouse	*une pension*	ewn pon·see·on
hotel	*un hôtel*	un o·tel
room in a private home	*une chambre chez un particulier*	ewn shom·brer shay zun par·tee·kew·lyay
youth hostel	*une auberge de jeunesse*	ewn o·bairzh der zher·nes

Can you recommend somewhere ...?	*Est-ce que vous pouvez recommander un logement ...?*	es·ker voo poo·vay rer·ko·mon·day un lozh·mon ...
cheap	*pas cher*	pa shair
nice	*agréable*	a·gray·a·bler
luxurlous	*luxueux*	lewk·sew·er
nearby	*près d'ici*	pray dee·see
romantic	*romantique*	ro·mon·teek

What's the address?
Quelle est l'adresse?　　　　　kel ay la·dres

For responses see **GO**, page 53.

Booking ahead & checking in

I'd like to book a room, please.
Je voudrais réserver   zher voo·dray ray·zair·vay
une chambre, s'il vous plaît.   ewn shom·brer seel voo play

I have a reservation.
J'ai une réservation.   zhay ewn ray·zair·va·syon

My name is ...
Mon nom est ...   mon nom ay ...

Do you have	*Avez-vous*	a·vay·voo
a ... room?	*une chambre ...?*	ewn shom·brer ...
double	*avec un grand lit*	a·vek ung gron lee
single	*à un lit*	a un lee
twin	*avec des lits*	a·vek day lee
	jumeaux	zhew·mo

How much	*Quel est*	kel ay
is it per ...?	*le prix par ...?*	ler pree par ...
night	*nuit*	nwee
person	*personne*	per·son
week	*semaine*	ser·men

I'd like to stay for (two) nights.
Je voudrais rester   zher voo·dray res·tay
pour (deux) nuits.   poor (der) nwee

From (July 2) to (July 6).
Du (deux juillet)   dew (der zhwee·yay)
au (six juillet).   o (see zhwee·yay)

There are (three) of us.
Nous sommes (trois).   noo som (trwa)

Can I see it?
Est-ce que je peux la voir?   es·ker zher per la vwar

SLEEP

It's fine, I'll take it.
C'est bien, je la prends.　　　say byun zher la pron

Do I need to pay upfront?
Est-ce qu'il faut payer par avance?　es·keel fo pay·yay par a·vons

Can I pay by ...?	*Est-ce qu'on peut payer avec ...?*	es·kom per pay·yay a·vek ...
credit card	*une carte de crédit*	ewn kart der kray·dee
travellers cheque	*des chèques de voyage*	day shek der vwa·yazh

Requests & queries

When/Where is breakfast served?
Quand/Où le petit déjeuner est-il servi?　kon/oo ler per·tee day·zher·nay ay·teel sair·vee

Please wake me at (seven).
Réveillez-moi à (sept) heures, s'il vous plaît.　ray·vay·yay·mwa a (set) er seel voo play

Could I have my key, please?
Puis-je avoir ma clé, s'il vous plaît.　pweezh av·war ma klay seel voo play

Could I have a receipt, please?
Puis-je avoir un reçu, s'il vous plaît?　pweezh av·war un v seel voo play

Can I use the ...?	*Est-ce que je peux utiliser ...?*	es·ker zher per ew·tee·lee·zay ...
kitchen	*la cuisine*	la kwee·zeen
laundry	*la blanchisserie*	la blon·shees·ree
telephone	*le téléphone*	ler tay·lay·fon

Do you have a/an ...?	Avez-vous ...?	a·vay·voo ...
elevator	un ascenseur	un a·son·ser
safe	un coffre-fort	ung ko·frer·for

Do you change money here?
Échangez-vous l'argent ici?   ay·shon·zhay·voo lar·zhon ee·see

Do you arrange tours here?
Organisez-vous des   or·ga·nee·zay·voo day
excursions ici?   zeks·kewr·syon ee·see

It's too ...	C'est trop ...	say tro ...
cold	froid	frwa
dark	sombre	som·brer
expensive	cher	shair
light/bright	clair	klair
noisy	bruyant	brew·yon
small	petit	per·tee

Can I get another ...?	Est-ce que je peux avoir un/une autre ...? m/f	es·ker zher per a·vwar un/ewn o·trer ...
This ... isn't clean.	Ce/Cette ... n'est pas propre. m/f	ser/set ... nay pa pro·prer
blanket	couverture f	koo·vair·tewr
pillow	oreiller m	o·ray·yay
pillowcase	taie f d'oreiller	tay do·ray·yay
sheet	drap m	drap
towel	serviette f	sair·vee·et

The ... doesn't work.	... ne fonctionne pas.	... ner fong·syon pa
air-conditioning	La climatisation	la klee·ma·tee·za·syon
fan	Le ventilateur	ler von·tee·la·ter
toilet	Les toilettes	lay twa·let
window	La fenêtre	la fer·ne·trer

Checking out

What time is checkout?
Quand faut-il régler?　　　　　　kon fo·teel ray·glay

Can I have a late checkout?
Pourrai je régler plus tard?　　poo·rezh ray·glay plew tar

Can I leave my luggage here until ...?	Puis-je laisser mes bagages jusqu'à ...?	pwee·zh lay say may ba·gazh zhews·ka ...
next week	la semaine prochaine	la ser·men pro·shen
tonight	ce soir	ser swar
Wednesday	mercredi	mair·krer·dee
Could I have my ..., please?	Est-ce que je pourrais avoir ..., s'il vous plaît?	es·ker zher poo·ray a·vwar ... seel voo play
deposit	ma caution	ma ko·syon
passport	mon passeport	mon pas·por
valuables	mes biens précieux	may byun pray·syer
I'll be back ...	Je retournerai ...	zher rer·toor·ner·ray ...
in (three) days	dans (trois) jours	don (trwa) zhur
on (Tuesday)	(mardi)	(mar·dee)

I had a great stay, thank you.
J'ai fait un séjour magnifique, merci.　　zhay fay un say·zhoor ma·nyee·feek mair·see

I'll recommend it to my friends.
Je le recommanderai à mes amis.　　zher ler rer·ko·mon·dray a may za·mee

WORK
Introductions

I'm attending a ...	Je participe à un/une ... m/f	zhe par·tee·seep a un/ewn ...
Where's the ...?	Où est le/la ...? m/f	oo ay ler/la ...
business centre	centre m d'affaires	son·trer da·fair
conference	conférence f	kon·fay·rons
course	stage m	stazh
meeting	réunion f	ray·ew·nyon
trade fair	foire f commerciale	fwar ko·mair·syal

I'm with ...	Je suis avec ...	zher swee a·vek ...
(the UN)	(l'ONU)	(lo en oo)
my colleague(s)	mon/ma collègue m/f	mong/ma ko·leg
	mes collègue(s) m&f pl	may ko·leg
(two) others	(deux) autres	(derz) o·trer

Here's my business card.
Voici ma carte. — vwa·see ma kart

Let me introduce my colleague.
Permettez-moi de vous présenter mon/ma collègue. m/f — pair·may·tay mwa de voo pray·zon·tay mon/ma ko·leg

I'm alone
Je suis seul(e). m/f — zher swee serl

I'm staying at ..., room ...
Je loge à ..., chambre ... — zher lozh a ... shom·brer ...

I'm here for (two) days/weeks.
Je suis ici pour (deux) jours/semaines. — zher swee·zee·see poor (der) zhoor/ser·men

Business needs

I have an appointment with ...
J'ai rendez-vous avec ... zhay ron·day·voo a·vek ...

I'm expecting a fax/call.
Je attends un fax/appel. zha·ton un faks/a·pel

I need an interpreter.
J'ai besoin d'un interprète. zhay ber·zwun dun un·tair·pret

I'd like ...	*Je voudrais ...*	zher voo·dray ...
a connection	*me connecter à*	mer ko·nek·tay a
to the internet	*l'internet*	lun·tair·net
to use a computer	*utiliser un*	ew·tee·lee·zay un
	ordinateur	or·dee·na·ter
to send an	*envoyer un*	en·vwa·yay un
email/fax	*email/fax*	e·mayl/faks

Is there a/an ...?	*Y a-t-il ...?*	ya·teel ...
data projector	*un projecteur data*	um pro·zhek·ter da·ta
laser pointer	*un pointeur laser*	un pwun·ter la·zair
overhead projector	*un rétroprojecteur*	un ray·tro·pro·zhek·ter
whiteboard	*un tableau blanc*	un ta·blo blon

After the deal

That went very well.
Ça s'est très bien passé. sa say tray byun pa·say

Shall we go for a drink?
On prend un verre? om pron tun vair

Shall we go for a meal?
On va manger? on va mon·zhay

It's on me.
C'est moi qui offre. say mwa kee o·frer

HELP
Emergencies

English	French	Pronunciation
Help!	*Au secours!*	o skoor
Stop!	*Arrêtez!*	a·ray·tay
Go away!	*Allez-vous-en!*	a·lay·voo·zon
Thief!	*Au voleur!*	o vo·ler
Fire!	*Au feu!*	o fer
Watch out!	*Faites attention!*	fet a·ton·syon

Call ...	*Appelez ...*	a·play ...
an ambulance	*une ambulance*	ewn omb·ew·lons
a doctor	*un médecin*	un mayd·sun
the fire brigade	*les pompiers*	lay pom·pyay
the police	*la police*	la po·lees

It's an emergency!
C'est urgent! — say tewr·zhon

Could you help me, please?
Est-ce que vous pourriez m'aider, s'il vous plaît? — es·ker voo poo·ryay may·day seel voo play

Could I use the telephone?
Est-ce que je pourrais utiliser le téléphone? — es·ker zher poo·ray ew·tee·lee·zay ler tay·lay·fon

I'm lost.
Je suis perdu(e). m/f — zher swee pair·dew

Where are the toilets?
Où sont les toilettes? — oo son lay twa·let

Leave me alone!
Laissez-moi tranquille! — lay·say·mwa trong·keel

Police

Where's the police station?
Où est le commissariat
de police?
oo ay ler ko·mee·sar·ya
der po·lees

I want to report an offence.
Je veux signaler un délit.
zher ver see·nya·lay un day·lee

I've been raped.
J'ai été violé(e). m/f
zhay ay·tay vyo·lay

I've been assaulted.
J'ai été violenté(e). m/f
zhay ay·tay vyo·lon·tay

I've been robbed.
On m'a volé.
on ma vo·lay

I want to contact my embassy/consulate.
Je veux contacter mon
ambassade/consulat.
zher ver kon·tak·tay mon
om·ba·sad/kon·sew·la

I've lost my ...	*J'ai perdu ...*	zhay pair·dew ...
My ... was/	*On m'a volé ...*	on ma vo·lay ...
were stolen.		
backpack	*mon sac à dos*	mon sak a do
bags	*mes valises*	may va·leez
credit card	*ma carte de crédit*	ma kart der kray·dee
handbag	*mon sac à main*	mon sak a mun
jewellery	*mes bijoux*	may bee·zhoo
money	*mon argent*	mon ar·zhon
passport	*mon passeport*	mom pas·por
travellers	*mes chèques*	may shek
cheques	*de voyage*	der vwa·yazh
wallet	*mon portefeuille*	mom por·ter·fer·yer

I have insurance.

Je suis assuré(e). m/f   zher sweez a·sew·ray

Can I have a receipt for my insurance?

Puis-je avoir le reçu   pweezh a·vwar ler rer·sew
pour mon assurance?   poor mon a·sew·rons

I have a prescription for this drug.

On m'a prescrit cette drogue.   om ma pray·skree set drog

Health

Where's a	*Où y a t-il*	oo ee a teel
nearby ...?	*un/une ... par ici?* m/f	un/ewn ... par ee·see
(night) chemist	*pharmacie* f	far·ma·see
	(de nuit)	(der nwee)
dentist	*dentiste* m&f	don·teest
doctor	*médecin* m&f	mayd·sun
hospital	*hôpital* m	o·pee·tal
medical centre	*centre* m	son·trer
	médical	may·dee·kal
optometrist	*optométriste* m&f	op·to·may·treest

I need a doctor (who speaks English).

J'ai besoin d'un médecin   zhay ber·zwun dun mayd·sun
(qui parle anglais).   (kee parl ong·glay)

Could I see a female doctor?

Est-ce que je peux voir   es·ker zher per vwar
une femme médecin?   ewn fam mayd·sun

Can the doctor come here?

Est-ce que le médecin   es·ker ler mayd·sun
peut venir ici?   per ver·neer ee·see

I've run out of my medication.
Je n'ai plus de médicaments.
zher nay plew der may·dee·ka·mon

My prescription is ...
Mon ordonnance indique ...
mo nor·do·nons on·deek ...

I've been vaccinated against ...	Je me suis fait vacciner contre ...	zher mer swee fay vak·see·nay kon·trer ...
hepatitis	l'hépatite	lay·pa·teet
tetanus	le tétanos	ler tay·ta·nos
typhoid	la typhoïde	la tee·fo·eed

I need new ...	J'ai besoin de nouvelles ...	zhay ber·zwun der noo·vel ...
contact lenses	lentilles de contact	lon·tee·yer der kon·takt
glasses	lunettes	lew·net

Symptoms, conditions & allergies

I'm sick.
Je suis malade.
zher swee ma·lad

I've been injured.
J'ai été blessé(e). m/f
zhay ay·tay blay·say

It hurts here.
J'ai une douleur ici.
zhay ewn doo·ler ee·see

I've been vomiting.
J'ai vomi.
zhay vo·mee

I can't sleep.
Je n'arrive pas à dormir.   zher na·reev pa a dor·meer

I feel ...	*Je me sens ...*	zher mer son ...
anxious	*inquiet/*	un·kyay/
	inquiète m/f	un·kyet
better	*mieux*	myer
weak	*faible*	fe·bler
worse	*plus mal*	plew mal

I feel ...	*J'ai ...*	zhay ...
dizzy	*des vertiges*	day ver·teezh
hot and cold	*chaud et froid*	sho ay frwa
nauseous	*des nausées*	day no·zay
shivery	*des frissons*	day free·son

I have (a/an) ...	*J'ai ...*	zhay ...
allergy	*une allergie*	ewn a·lair·zhee
asthma	*de l'asthme*	de las·mer
bronchitis	*une bronchite*	ewn bron·sheet
cold	*un rhume*	un rewm
cough	*une toux*	ewn too
diabetes	*du diabète*	dew dya·bet
diarrhoea	*la diarrhée*	la dya·ray
fever	*de la fièvre*	der la fyay·vrer
headache	*mal à la tête*	mal a la tet
heart condition	*une condition*	ewn kon·dee·syon
	cardiaque	kar·dyak
sore throat	*mal à la gorge*	mal a la gorzh
swelling	*un gonflement*	un gon·fler·mon
venereal	*une maladie*	ewn ma·la·dee
disease	*vénérienne*	vay·nay·ryen

I've recently had ...
J'ai eu récemment ...   zhay ew ray·sa·mon ...

I'm on medication for ...
Je prends des   zher pron day
médicaments pour ...   may·dee·ka·mon poor ...

I need something for ...
J'ai besoin d'un   zhay ber·zwun dun
médicament pour ...   may·dee·ka·mom poor ...

Do I need a prescription for ...?
J'ai besoin d'une   zhay ber·zwun dewn
ordonnance pour ...?   or·do·nons poor ...

How many times a day?
Combien de fois par jour? kom·byun der fwa par zhoor

I'm allergic to ...	*Je suis*	zher swee
	allergique ...	za·lair·zheek ...
antibiotics	*aux antibiotiques*	o zon·tee·byo·teek
anti-	*aux anti-*	o zun·tee·
inflammatories	*inflammatoires*	un·fla·ma·twar
aspirin	*à l'aspirine*	a las·pee·reen
bees	*aux abeilles*	o za·bay·yer
codeine	*à la codéine*	a la ko·day·een
penicillin	*à la pénicilline*	a la payn·nee·
		see·leen
pollen	*au pollen*	o po·len

I have a skin allergy.
J'ai une allergie de peau.   zhay ewn a·lair·zhee der po

For food-related allergies, see **EAT & DRINK**, page 40.

Numbers

0	*zéro*	zay·ro		18	*dix-huit*	dee·zweet
1	*un*	un		19	*dix-neuf*	deez·nerf
2	*deux*	der		20	*vingt*	vung
3	*trois*	trwa		21	*vingt et un*	vung tay un
4	*quatre*	ka·trer		22	*vingt-deux*	vung·der
5	*cinq*	sungk		30	*trente*	tront
6	*six*	sees		40	*quarante*	ka·ront
7	*sept*	set		50	*cinquante*	sung·kont
8	*huit*	weet		60	*soixante*	swa·sont
9	*neuf*	nerf		70	*soixante-dix*	swa·son·dees
10	*dix*	dees		71	*soixante-et-onze*	swa·sont·et·onz
11	*onze*	onz		80	*quatre-vingts*	ka·trer·vung
12	*douze*	dooz		90	*quatre-vingt-*	ka·trer·vung·
13	*treize*	trez			*dix*	dees
14	*quatorze*	ka·torz				
15	*quinze*	kunz	100	*cent*	son	
16	*seize*	sez	1,000	*mille*	meel	
17	*dix-sept*	dee·set	1,000,000	*un million*	um meel·yon	

Colours

black	*noir(e)*	nwar		pink	*rose*	roz
blue	*bleu(e)*	bler		purple	*violet/*	vyo·lay/
brown	*brun/*	brun/			*violette*	vyo·let
	brune	brewn		red	*rouge*	roozh
green	*vert(e)*	vair(t)		white	*blanc(he)*	blon(sh)
orange	*orange*	o·ronzh		yellow	*jaune*	zhon

Time & dates

What time is it?	*Quelle heure est-il?*	kel er ay·teel
It's (one) o'clock.	*Il est (une) heure.*	ee·lay (ewn) er
It's (10) o'clock.	*Il est (dix) heures.*	ee·lay (deez) er
Quarter past one.	*Il est une heure et quart.*	ee·lay ewn eray kar
Twenty past one.	*Il est une heure vingt.*	ee·lay ewn er vung
Half past one.	*Il est une heure et demie.*	ee·lay ewn er ay der·mee
Twenty to one.	*Il est une heure moins vingt.*	ee·lay ewn er mwun vung
Quarter to one.	*Il est une heure moins le quart*	ee·lay ewn er mwun ler kar
At what time?	*À quelle heure?*	a kel er

Monday	*lundi*	lun·dee
Tuesday	*mardi*	mar·dee
Wednesday	*mercredi*	mair·krer·dee
Thursday	*jeudi*	zher·dee
Friday	*vendredi*	von·drer·dee
Saturday	*samedi*	sam·dee
Sunday	*dimanche*	dee·monsh

January	*janvier*	zhon·vyay
February	*février*	fayv·ryay
March	*mars*	mars
April	*avril*	a·vreel
May	*mai*	may
June	*juin*	zhwun
July	*juillet*	zhwee·yay
August	*août*	oot
September	*septembre*	sep·tom·brer
October	*octobre*	ok·to·brer
November	*novembre*	no·vom·brer
December	*décembre*	day·som·brer

spring	*printemps* m	prun·tom
summer	*été* m	ay·tay
autumn	*automne* m	o·ton
winter	*hiver* m	ee·vair

What date?
Quelle date? kel dat

What's today's date?
C'est quel jour aujourd'hui? say kel zhoor o·zhoor·dwee

It's (18 October).
C'est le (dix-huit octobre). say ler (dee·zwee tok·to·brer)

last ...

month	*le mois dernier*	ler mwa dair·nyay
night	*hier soir*	ee·yair swar
week	*la semaine dernière*	la ser·men dair·nyair
year	*l'année dernière*	la·nay dair·nyair

next ...

month	*le mois prochain*	ler mwa pro·shen
week	*la semaine prochaine*	la se·men pro·shen
year	*l'année prochaine*	la·nay pro·shen

since (May) *depuis (mai)* der·pwee (may)

tomorrow ... *demain ...* der·mun ...

afternoon	*après-midi*	a·pray·mee·dee
evening	*soir*	swar
morning	*matin*	ma·tun

yesterday ... *hier ...* ee·yair ...

afternoon	*après-midi*	a·pray·mee·dee
evening	*soir*	swar
morning	*matin*	ma·tun

Nouns in this dictionary have their gender indicated by m (masculine) or f (feminine).
If it's a plural noun, you'll also see pl.
Where no gender is marked the word is either an adjective or a verb, with adjectives first.

A

aboard *à bord* a bor
accident *accident* m ak·see·don
accommodation *logement* m lozh·mon
account *compte* m kont
adaptor *adaptateur* m a·dap·ta·ter
address *adresse* f a·dres
admission (price) *prix* m *d'entrée* pree don·tray
after *après* a·pray
afternoon *après-midi* m a·pray·mee·dee
aftershave *après-rasage* m a·pray·ra·zazh
again *encore* ong·kor
air-conditioned *climatisé(e)* m/f klee·ma·tee·zay
airline *ligne f aérienne* lee·nyer a·ay·ryen
airmail *par avion* par a·vyon
airplane *avion* m a·vyon
airport *aéroport* m a·ay·ro·por
aisle (on plane, etc) *couloir* m koo·lwar
alarm clock *réveil* m ray·vay
alcohol *alcool* m al·kol
all *tout(e)* too(t)
allergy *allergie* f a·lair·zhee
almonds *amandes* f pl a·mond
alone *tout(e) seul(e)* m/f too(t) serl
ambulance *ambulance* f om·bew·lons
American *américain/américaine* m/f a·may·ree·kun/a·may·ree·ken and et ay
ankle *cheville* f sher·vee·yer
another *un/une autre* m/f un/ewn o·trer
antibiotics *antibiotiques* m pl on·tee·byo·teek
antiseptic *antiseptique* m on·tee·sep·teek
apartment *appartement* m a·par·ter·mon
apple *pomme* f pom
appointment *rendez-vous* m ron·day·voo
apricot *abricot* m a·bree·ko

architect *architecte* m&f ar·shee·tekt
architecture *architecture* f ar·shee·tek·tewr
arm *bras* m bra
arrivals *arrivées* f pl a·ree·vay
art *art* m ar
art gallery *musée* m • *galerie* f mew·zay • gal·ree
artist *artiste* m&f ar·teest
ashtray *cendrier* m son·dree·yay
aspirin *aspirine* f as·pee·reen
at *à* a
aunt *tante* f tont
Australia *Australie* f o·stra·lee
autumn *automne* m o·ton
automatic teller machine (ATM) *guichet* m *automatique de banque (GAB)* gee·shay o·to·ma·teek der bonk

B

B&W (film) *noir et blanc* nwar ay blong
baby *bébé* m bay·bay
baby food *bouillie* f boo·yee
babysitter *baby-sitter* m&f ba·bee·see·ter
back (body) *dos* m do
backpack *sac* m *à dos* sak a do
bacon *lard* m lar
bad *mauvais(e)* m/f mo·vay(z)
bag *sac* m sak
baggage *bagages* m pl ba·gazh
baggage allowance *franchise* f fron·sheez
baggage claim *retrait* m *des bagages* rer·tray day ba·gazh
bakery *boulangerie* f boo·lon·zhree
banana *banane* f ba·nan
band (music) *bande* f bond
bandage *pansement* m pons·mon

Band-Aid *sparadrap* m spa·ra·dra
bank *banque* f bonk
bank account *compte* m *bancaire* kont bong·kair
banknote *billet* m *de banque* bee·yay der bonk
bar *bar* m bar
bath *baignoire* f be·nywar
bathroom *salle* f *de bain* sal der bun
battery *pile* f peel
beach *plage* f plazh
beans (French) *haricots* m pl *verts* a·ree·ko ver
beautiful *beau/belle* m/f bo/bel
beauty salon *salon* m *de beauté* sa·lon der bo·tay
bed *lit* m lee
bed linen *draps* m pl dra
bedroom *chambre* f *à coucher* shom·brer a koo·shay
beef *bœuf* m berf
beer *bière* f byair
before *avant* a·von
behind *derrière* dair·yair
beside *à côté de* a ko·tay der
best *le/la meilleur(e)* m/f ler/la may·yer
better *meilleur(e)* m/f may·yer
bicycle *vélo* m vay·lo
big *grand(e)* m/f gron(d)
bigger *plus grand(e)* m/f plew gron(d)
biggest *le/la plus grand(e)* m/f ler/la plew gron(d)
bill (restaurant) *addition* f a·dee·syon
birthday *anniversaire* m a·nee·vair·sair
bitter *amer/amère* m/f a·mair
blanket *couverture* f koo·vair·tewr
blister *ampoule* f om·pool
blocked *bloqué(e)* m/f blo·kay
blood *sang* m son
blood group *groupe* m *sanguin* groop song·gun
board (a plane, ship) *monter à bord* mon·tay a bor

boarding house *pension* f pon·syon
boarding pass *carte* f *d'embarquement* kart dom·bar·ker·mon
boat *bateau* m ba·to
book *livre* m leev·rer
book (make a booking) *réserver* ray·zair·vay
booked up *complet/complète* m/f kom·play/kom·plet
bookshop *librairie* f lee·bray·ree
boots *bottes* f pl bot
border *frontière* f fron·tyair
boring *ennuyeux/ennuyeuse* m/f on·nwee·yer/on·nwee·yerz
both *tous les deux* too lay der
bottle *bouteille* f boo·tay
bottle opener *ouvre-bouteille* m oo·vrer·boo·tay
bowl *bol* m bol
box *boîte* f bwat
boy *garçon* m gar·son
boyfriend *petit ami* m per·tee a·mee
bra *soutien-gorge* m soo·tyung·gorzh
brakes *freins* m frun
bread *pain* m pun
breakfast *petit déjeuner* m per·tee day·zher·nay
bridge *pont* m pon
briefcase *serviette* f sair·vyet
brochure *brochure* f bro·shewr
broken *cassé(e)* m/f ka·say
broken down (tombé) en panne (tom·bay) on pan
brother *frère* m frair
brown *brun/brune* m/f brun/brewn
brush *brosse* f bros
budget *budget* m bew·dzay
buffet *buffet* m bew·fay
building *bâtiment* m ba·tee·mon
burn *brûlure* f brew·lewr
bus (city) *(auto)bus* m (o·to)bews
bus (intercity) *(auto)car* m (o·to)kar
bus station *gare* f *routière* gar roo·tyair
bus stop *arrêt* m *d'autobus* a·ray do·to·bews

English–French dictionary C

business *affaires* f pl a·fair
business class *classe f d'affaires* klas a·fair
business man/woman *homme/femme m/f d'affaires* om/fam da·fair
business trip *voyage m d'affaires* vwa·yazh da·fair
busy *occupé(e)* m/f o·kew·pay
butcher's shop *boucherie* f boosh·ree
butter *beurre* m ber
button *bouton* m boo·ton
buy *acheter* ash·tay

C

cabbage *chou* m shoo
café *café* m ka·fay
cake shop *pâtisserie* f pa·tees·ree
calculator *calculatrice* f kal·kew·la·treez
call *appeler* a·pe·lay
camera *appareil m photo* a·pa·ray fo·to
camping ground *camping* m kom·peeng
camp site *terrain m de camping* tay·run der kom·peeng
can (tin) *boîte* f bwat
can opener *ouvre-boîte* m oo·vrer·bwat
Canada *Canada* m ka·na·da
cancel *annuler* a·new·lay
capsicum *polvron* m pwa·vron
car *voiture* f vwa·tewr
car hire *location f de voitures* lo·ka·syon der vwa·tewr
car owner's title *carte f grise* kart greez
car registration *immatriculation* ee·ma·tree·kew·la·syon
carpark *parking* m par·keeng
carrot *carotte* f ka·rot
cash *argent* m ar·zhon
cash (a cheque) *encaisser* ong·kay·say
cash register *caisse f (enregistreuse)* kes (on·rer·zhee·strerz)
cashier *caissier/caissière* m/f ke·syay/ke·syair
cassette *cassette* f ka·set

castle *château* m sha·to
cathedral *cathédrale* f ka·tay·dral
CD *CD* m say·day
centre *centre* m son·trer
cereal *céréales* m pl say·ray·al
chair *chaise* f shez
chairlift (skiing) *télésiège* m tay·lay·syezh
champagne *champagne* m shom·pa·nyer
change (coins) *monnaie* f mo·nay
change (money) *échanger* ay·shon·zhay
change (general) *changer* shon·zhay
changing room *cabine f d'essayage* ka·been day·say·yazh
cheap *bon marché* f bon mar·shay
check (banking) *chèque* m shek
check (bill) *addition* f a·dee·syon
check-in (desk) *enregistrement* on·rer·zhee·strer·mon
cheese *fromage* m fro·mazh
chef *chef m de cuisine* shef der kwee·zeen
chemist (place) *pharmacie* f far·ma·see
chemist (person) *pharmacien(ne)* m/f far·ma·syun/far·ma·syen
cheque (banking) *chèque* m shek
cherry *cerises* f se·reez
chest *poitrine* f pwa·treen
chicken *poulet* m poo·lay
child *enfant* m/f on·fon
child seat *siège m pour enfant* syezh poor on·fon
childminding *garderie* f gard·ree
children *enfants* m/f pl on·fon
chocolate *chocolat* m sho·ko·la
Christmas *Noël* m no·el
church *église* f ay·gleez
cigar *cigare* m see·gar
cigarette *cigarette* f see·ga·ret
cigarette lighter *briquet* m bree·kay
cinema *cinéma* m see·nay·ma
circus *cirque* m seerk
city *ville* f veel
city centre *centre-ville* m son·trer·veel
clean *propre* pro·prer
clean *nettoyer* net·wa·yay

cleaning *nettoyage* m net-wa-yazh
client *client(e)* m/f klee-on(t)
cloakroom *vestiaire* m vays-tyair
close *près* pray
close *fermer* fair-may
closed *fermé(e)* m/f fair-may
clothing *vêtements* m pl vet-mon
clothing store *magasin* m *de vêtements* ma-ga-zun der vet-mon
coat *manteau* m mon-to
cocktail *cocktail* m kok-tel
coffee *café* m ka-fay
coins *pièces* f pl pyes
cold *froid(e)* m/f frwa(d)
colleague *collègue* m/f ko-leg
collect call *appel* m en PCV a-pel on pay-say-vay
colour *couleur* f koo-ler
comb *peigne* m pe-nyer
comfortable *confortable* kon-for-ta-bler
companion *compagnon/compagne* m/f kom-pa-nyon/kom-pa-nyer
company *entreprise* f on-trer-preez
complaint *plainte* f plunt
complimentary (free) *gratuit(e)* m/f gra-twee(t)
computer *ordinateur* m or-dee-na-ter
concert *concert* m kon-sair
concussion *commotion* f *cérébrale* ko-mo-syon say-ray-bral
conditioner (hair) *après-shampooing* m a-pray-shom-pwung
condom *préservatif* m pray-zair-va-teef
conference (big) *congrès* m kong-gray
conference (small) *colloque* m ko-lok
confirm (a booking) *confirmer* kon-feer-may
congratulations *félicitations* fay-lee-see-ta-syon
connection *rapport* m ra-por
constipation *constipation* f kon-stee-pa-syon
consulate *consulat* m kon-sew-la
contact lenses *verres de contact* m pl vair der kon-takt

convenience store *supérette* f *de quartier* sew-pay-ret der kar-tyay
cook *cuisinier/cuisinière* m/f kwee-zee-nyay/kwee-zee-nyair
cook *cuire* kweer
cool *frais/fraîche* m/f fray/fresh
corkscrew *tire-bouchon* m teer-boo-shon
cost *coût* m koo
cotton *coton* m ko-ton
cotton balls *ouate* f *de coton* wat der ko-ton
cough *toux* f too
cough medicine *sirop* m *contre la toux* see-ro kon-trer la too
countryside *campagne* f kom-pa-nyer
court (tennis) *court* m koor
cover charge *couvert* m koo-vair
crafts *artisanat* m ar-tee-za-na
cream *crème* f krem
crèche *crèche* f kresh
credit *crédit* m kray-dee
credit card *carte de crédit* kart der kray-dee
cup *tasse* f tas
currency exchange *taux m de change* to der shonzh
current (electricity) *courant* m koo-ron
custom *coutume* f koo-tewm
customs *douane* f dwan
cutlery *couverts* m pl koo-vair

D

daily *quotidien(ne)* m/f ko-tee-dyun/ko-tee-dyen
dance f *danse* dons
dance *danser* don-say
dancing *danse* f dons
dangerous *dangereux/dangereuse* m/f don-zhrer/don-zhrerz
dark *obscur(e)* m/f ob-skewr
dark (of colour) *foncé(e)* m/f fon-say
date (day) *date* f dat

date of birth *date* f *de naissance* dat der nay·sons

daughter *fille* f fee·yer

dawn *aube* f ob

day *jour* m zhoor

day after tomorrow (the) *après-demain* a·pray·der·mun

day before yesterday (the) *avant-hier* a·von·tyair

delay *retard* m rer·tard

delicatessen *traiteur* m tre·ter

deliver *livrer* leev·ray

dental floss *fil* m *dentaire* feel don·tair

dentist *dentiste* m&f don·teest

deodorant *déodorant* m day·o·do·ron

depart (leave) *partir* par·teer

department store *grand magasin* m gron ma·ga·zun

departure *départ* m day·par

deposit *dépôt* m day·po

destination *destination* f des·tee·na·syon

diabetes *diabète* m dya·bet

dial tone *tonalité* f to·na·lee·tay

diaper *couche* f koosh

diarrhoea *diarrhée* f dya·ray

diary *agenda* m a·zhun·da

dictionary *dictionnaire* m deek·syo·nair

different *différent(e)* m/f dee·fay·ron(t)

dinner *dîner* m dee·nay

direct *direct(e)* m/f dee·rekt

direct-dial *composition* f *directe* kom·po·zees·yon dee·rekt

direction *direction* f dee·rek·syon

dirty *sale* sal

disabled *handicapé(e)* m/f on·dee·ka·pay

discount *remise* f rer·meez

dish *plat* m pla

disk (CD-ROM) *disque* m deesk

disk (floppy) *disquette* f dees·ket

doctor *médecin* m&f mayd·sun

dog *chien* m shyun

dollar *dollar* m do·lar

dope (drugs) *drogue* f drog

double bed *grand lit* m gron lee

double room *chambre* f *pour deux personnes* shom·brer poor der pair·son

dress *robe* f rob

drink *boisson* f bwa·son

drink *boire* bwar

drink (alcoholic) *verre* m vair

drive *conduire* kon·dweer

drivers licence *permis* m *de conduire* pair·mee der kon·dweer

drug *drogue* f drog

drunk *ivre* ee·vrer

dry *sec/sèche* m/f sek/sesh

dry *sécher* say·shay

duck *canard* m

dummy (pacifier) *tétine* f tay·teen

E

each *chaque* shak

ear *oreille* f o·ray

early *tôt* to

earrings *boucles* f pl *d'oreille* boo·kler do·ray

east *est* m est

Easter *Pâques* pak

eat *manger* mon·zhay

economy class *classe* f *touriste* klas too·reest

egg *œuf* m erf

electrical store *magasin* m *qui vend des appareils électriques* ma·ga·zun kee von day za·pa·ray ay·lek·treek

electricity *électricité* f ay·lek·tree·see·tay

elevator *ascenseur* m a·son·ser

email *e-mail* m ay·mel

embassy *ambassade* f om·ba·sad

emergency *cas* m *urgent* ka ewr·zhon

empty *vide* veed

end *finir* fee·neer

engaged *fiancé(e)* m/f fyon·say

engagement *fiançailles* f pl fyon·sai

engine *moteur* m mo·ter

engineer *ingénieur* m un-zhay-nyer
engineering *ingénierie* f un-zhay-nee-ree
England *Angleterre* f ong-gler-tair
English *anglais(e)* m/f ong-glay(z)
enough *assez* a-say
enter *entrer* on-tray
entertainment guide *programme* m *des spectacles* pro-gram day spek-tak-ler
entry *entrée* f on-tray
envelope *enveloppe* f on-vlop
escalator *escalier* m *roulant* es-ka-lyay roo-lon
estate agency *agence* f *immobilière* a-zhons ee-mo-bee-lyair
euro *euro* m er-ro
Europe *Europe* f er-rop
evening *soir* m swar
every *chaque* shak
everyone *tout le monde* too ler mond
everything *tout* too
exactly *exactement* eg-zak-ter-mon
excess (baggage) *excédent* ek-say-don
exchange *échange* m ay-shonzh
exchange *échanger* ay-shon-zhay
exchange rate *taux* m *de change* to der shonzh
exhibition *exposition* f ek-spo-zee-syon
exit *sortie* f sor-tee
expensive *cher/chère* m/f shair
express (mail) *exprès* eks-pres
eye *œil* m er-yee
eyes *yeux* m yer

F

face *visage* m vee-zazh
fall (autumn) *automne* m o-ton
family *famille* f fa-mee-yer
family name *nom* m *de famille* non der fa-mee-yer
fan (machine) *ventilateur* m von-tee-la-ter
far *loin* lwun

fare *tarif* m ta-reef
fashion *mode* f mod
fast *rapide* ra-peed
fat *gras(se)* m/f gra(s)
father *père* m pair
faucet *robinet* m ro-bee-nay
faulty *défectueux/défectueuse* m/f day-fek-twer/day-fek-twerz
fax *fax* m faks
feel (touch) *toucher* too-shay
feeling (physical) *sensation* f son-sa-syon
female *femelle* fer-mel
ferry *bac* m bak
fever *fièvre* f fyev-rer
fiancé *fiancé* m fyon-say
fiancée *fiancée* f fyon-say
film (cinema) *film* m feelm
film (for camera) *pellicule* f pay-lee-kewl
film speed *sensibilité* f *de la pellicule* son-see-bee-lee-tay der la pay-lee-kewl
fine (penalty) *amende* f a-mond
finger *doigt* m dwa
first class *première classe* f prer-myair klas
first-aid kit *trousse* f *à pharmacie* troos a far-ma-see
fish *poisson* f pwa-son
fish shop *poissonnerie* f pwa-son-ree
fishing *pêche* f pesh
flashlight *lampe* f *de poche* lomp der posh
fleamarket *marché* m *aux puces* mar-shay o pews
flight *vol* m vol
floor (storey) *étage* m ay-tazh
florist *fleuriste* m/f fler-reest
flu *grippe* f greep
fly *mouche* f moosh
food *nourriture* f noo-ree-tewr
foot *pied* m pyay
football (soccer) *football* m foot-bol
footpath *sentier* m son-tyay
foreign *étranger/étrangère* m/f ay-tron-zhay/ay-tron-zhair

forest *forêt* f fo·ray
fork *fourchette* f foor·shet
fortnight *quinze jours* m pl kunz zhoor
fragile *fragile* fra·zheel
France *la France* f la frons
free (available) *disponible* dees·po·nee·bler
free (gratis) *gratuit(e)* m/f gra·twee(t)
French *Français(e)* m/f fron·say(z)
fresh *frais/fraîche* m/f fray/fresh
fridge *réfrigérateur* m ray·free·zhay·ra·ter
friend *ami(e)* m/f a·mee
from *de* der
frozen *gelé(e)* m/f zher·lay
fruit *fruit* m frwee
fry *faire frire* fair freer
frying pan *poêle* f pwal
full *plein(e)* m/f plun/plen
funny *drôle* m/f drol
furniture *meubles* m pl mer·bler

G

game (football) *match* m matsh
garbage can *poubelle* f poo·bel
garden *jardin* m zhar·dun
gas (for cooking) *gaz* m gaz
gas (petrol) *essence* f ay·sons
gastroenteritis *gastro-entérite* f gastro·on·tay·reet
gay *homosexuel(le)* m/f o·mo·sek·swel
Germany *Allemagne* f al·ma·nyer
get off (a train, etc) *descendre* day·son·drer
gift *cadeau* m ka·do
gig *concert* m kon·sair
girl *fille* f fee·yer
girlfriend *petite amie* f per·teet a·mee
glass *verre* m vair
glasses (spectacles) *lunettes* f pl lew·net
gloves *gants* m pl gon
go *aller* a·lay
go out *sortir* sor·teer
gold *or* m or
golf course *terrain de golf* m tay·run der golf

good *bon/bonne* m/f bon/bon
goodbye *au revoir* o rer·vwar
gram *gramme* m gram
grandchild *petit-fils/petite-fille* m/f per·tee fees/per·teet fee·yer
grandfather *grand-père* m grom·pair
grandmother *grand-mère* f grom·mair
grapes *raisins* m pl ray·sun
grateful *reconnaissant(e)* m/f rer·ko·nay·son(t)
great (fantastic) *génial(e)* m/f zhay·nyal
grocery *épicerie* f ay·pee·sree
guaranteed *garanti(e)* m/f ga·ron·tee
guesthouse *pension* f (de famille) pon·syon (der fa·mee·yer)
guide (person) *guide* m geed
guidebook *guide* m geed
guided tour *visite guidée* vee·zeet gee·day
gym *gymnase* m zheem·naz

H

haircut *coupe* f koop
hairdresser *coiffeur/coiffeuse* m/f kwa·fer/kwa·ferz
half *moitié* f mwa·tyay
hand *main* f mun
handbag *sac à main* sak a mun
handicrafts *objets* m pl *artisanaux* ob·zhay ar·tee·za·no
handkerchief *mouchoir* m moo·shwar
handmade *fait/faite à la main* m/f fay/fet a la mun
handsome *beau/belle* m/f bo/bel
happy *heureux/heureuse* m/f er·rer/er·rerz
hard (not soft) *dur(e)* m/f dewr
hat *chapeau* m sha·po
have *avoir* a·vwar
hay fever *rhume* m *des foins* rewm day fwun
he *il* eel
head *tête* f tet
headache *mal* m *à la tête* mal a la tet
headlights *phares* m pl far

English–French dictionary

heart *cœur* m ker
heart condition *maladie* f *de cœur* ma-la-dee der ker
heat *chaleur* f sha-ler
heated *chauffé(e)* m/f sho-fay
heater *appareil* m *de chauffage* a-pa-ray der sho-fazh
heavy *lourd(e)* m/f loor(d)
help *aider* ay-day
help *aide* f ed
her *son/sa/ses* m/f/pl son/sa/say
here *ici* ee-see
high *haut(e)* m/f o(t)
highway *autoroute* f o-to-root
hike *faire la randonnée* fair la ron-do-nay
hiking *randonnée* f ron-do-nay
hire *louer* loo-ay
his *son/sa/ses* m/f/pl son/sa/say
hitchhike *faire du stop* fair dew stop
holidays *vacances* f pl va-kons
home *à la maison* a la may-zon
homosexual *homosexuel(le)* m/f o-mo-sek-swel
honeymoon *lune* f *de miel* lewn der myel
horse riding *équitation* f ay-kee-ta-syon
hospital *hôpital* m o-pee-tal
hot *chaud(e)* m/f sho(d)
hotel *hôtel* m o-tel
hour *heure* f er
hungry (to be) *avoir faim* a-vwar fum
husband *mari* m ma-ree

I

I *je* zher
ice *glace* f glas
ice cream *glace* f glas
identification card (ID) *carte* f *d'identité* kart dee-don-tee-tay
ill *malade* ma-lad
important *important(e)* m/f um-por-ton(t)
impossible *impossible* um-po-see-bler
in *dans* don

in a hurry *pressé(e)* m/f pray-say
included *compris(e)* m/f kom-pree(z)
indigestion *indigestion* f un-dee-zhes-tyon
infection *infection* f un-fek-syon
influenza *grippe* f greep
information *renseignements* m pl ron-sen-yer-mon
injection *piqûre* f pee-kewr
injured *blessé(e)* m/f blay-say
injury *blessure* f blay-sewr
insurance *assurance* f a-sew-rons
intermission *entracte* m on-trakt
Internet *Internet* m un-tair-net
Internet café *cybercafé* m see-bair-ka-fay
Ireland *Irlande* f eer-lond
iron (for clothes) *fer* m *à repasser* fair a rer-pa-say
island *île* f eel
IT *informatique* f un-for-ma-teek
Italy *Italie* f ee-ta-lee
itch *démangeaison* f day-mon-zhay-zon
itinerary *itinéraire* m ee-tee-nay-rair

J

jacket *veste* f vest
jam *confiture* f kon-fee-tewr
jeans *jean* m zheen
jet lag *fatigue* f *due au décalage horaire* fa-teeg dew o day-ka-lazh o-rair
jewellery *bijoux* m pl bee-zhoo
job *travail* m tra-vai
journey *voyage* m vwa-yazh
jumper (sweater) *pull* m pewl

K

key *clé* f klay
kilo *kilo* m kee-lo
kilogram *kilogramme* m kee-lo-gram
kilometre *kilomètre* m kee-lo-may-trer

kind (nice) *gentil(le)* m/f zhon·tee
kiosk *kiosque* m kyosk
kitchen *cuisine* f kwee·zeen
knee *genou* m zhnoo
knife *couteau* m koo·to

L

lake *lac* m lak
lamb *agneau* m a·nyo
language *langue* f longk
laptop *ordinateur* m *portable*
   or dee·na·ter por·ta·bler
last (previous) *dernier/dernière* m/t
   dair·nyay/dair·nyair
late *en retard* on rer·tar
later *plus tard* plew·tar
launderette *laverie* f lav·ree
laundry (place) *blanchisserie* f
   blon·shees·ree
laundry (clothes) *linge* m lunzh
law (study, profession) *droit* m drwa
lawyer *avocat(e)* m/f a·vo·ka(t)
laxative *laxatif* m lak·sa·teef
leather *cuir* m kweer
left (direction) *à gauche* a gosh
left luggage (office) *consigne* f kon·see·nyer
leg *jambe* f zhomb
lemon *citron* m pl see·tron
lens *objectif* m ob·zhek·teef
lesbian *lesbienne* f les·byen
less *moins* mwun
letter *lettre* f lay·trer
lettuce *laitue* f lay·tew
library *bibliothèque* f bee·blee·o·tek
life jacket *gilet* m *de sauvetage* zhee·lay
   der sov·tazh
lift (elevator) *ascenseur* m a·son·ser
light *lumière* f lew·myair
light (not heavy) *léger/légère* m/f
   lay·zhay/lay·zhair
light (of colour) *clair(e)* m/f klair
light meter *posemètre* m poz·may·trer

lighter *briquet* m bree·kay
like *comme* kom
linen (material) *lin* m lun
linen (sheets etc) *linge* m lunzh
lipstick *rouge* m *à lèvres* roozh a lay·vrer
liquor store *magasin* m *de vins et spiritueux*
   ma·ga·zun der vun ay spee·ree·twer
listen (to) *écouter* ay·koo·tay
little bit *peu* m per
lobster *homard* m o·mar
local *local(e)* m/f lo·kal
lock *fermer à clé* fair·may a klay
locked *fermé(e) à clé* m/f fair·may a klay
long *long(ue)* m/f long(k)
lost *perdu(e)* m/f pair·dew
lost property office *bureau* m *des objets*
   trouvés bew·ro day zob·zhay troo·vay
loud *fort(e)* m/f for(t)
love *amour* a·moor
love *aimer* ay·may
lubricant *lubrifiant* m lew·bree·fyoñ
luggage *bagages* m pl ba·gazh
luggage lockers *consigne* f *automatique*
   kon·see·nyer o·to·ma·teek
lunch *déjeuner* m day zher·nay
luxury *de luxe* der lewks

M

mail (letters) *courrier* m koo·ryay
mail (postal system) *poste* f post
mailbox *boîte* f *aux lettres* bwat o lay·trer
make-up *maquillage* m ma·kee·yazh
man *homme* m om
manager (restaurant, hotel) *gérant(e)*
   m/f zhay·ron(t)
map (of country) *carte* f kart
map (of town) *plan* m plon
market *marché* m mar·shay
married *marié(e)* m/f ma·ryay
massage *massage* m ma·sazh
masseur/masseuse *masseur/masseuse*
   m/f ma·ser/ma·serz

match (sports) *match* m matsh
matches (for lighting) *allumettes* f pl
a·lew·met
mattress *matelas* m mat·la
me *moi* mwa
meal *repas* m rer·pa
meat *viande* f vyond
medicine *médecine* f med·seen
medicine (medication) *médicament* m
may·dee·ka·mon
menu *carte* kart
message *message* m may·sazh
metre *mètre* m may·trer
metro station *station* f *de métro* sta·syon
der may·tro
microwave (oven) *four* m à *micro-ondes*
foor a mee·kro·ond
midday/noon *midi* mee·dee
midnight *minuit* mee·nwee
milk *lait* m lay
millimetre *millimètre* m mee·lee·may·trer
mineral water *eau* f *minérale*
o mee·nay·ral
minute *minute* f mee·newt
mirror *miroir* m mee·rwar
Miss *Mademoiselle* mad·mwa·zel
mobile phone *téléphone* m *portable*
tay·lay·fon por·ta·bler
modem *modem* m mo·dem
modern *moderne* mo·dairn
money *argent* m ar·zhon
month *mois* m mwa
more *plus* plew
morning *matin* m ma·tun
motel *motel* m mo·tel
mother *mère* f mair
motorcycle *moto* m mo·to
motorway (tollway) *autoroute* f o·to·root
mountain *montagne* f mon·ta·nyer
mouth *bouche* f boosh
movie *film* m feelm
Mr *Monsieur* mer·syer
Mrs *Madame* ma·dam

Ms *Mademoiselle* mad·mwa·zel
museum *musée* m mew·zay
muesli *muesli* m mewz·lee
music *musique* f mew·zeek
music shop *disquaire* m dee·skair
my *mon/ma/mes* m/f/pl mon/ma/may

N

nail clippers *coupe-ongles* m koop·ong·gler
name (general) *nom* m nom
name (first/given) *prénom* m pray·non
napkin *serviette* f sair·vyet
nappy *couche* f koosh
nausea *nausée* f no·zay
near *près de* pray der
nearby *tout près* too pray
nearest *le/la plus proche* m/f ler/la plew
prosh
necklace *collier* m ko·lyay
needle *aiguille* f ay·gwee·yer
Netherlands *Pays-Bas* m pl pay·ee·ba
new *nouveau/nouvelle* m/f noo·vo/
noo·vel
New Year's Day *jour* m *de l'An* zhoor der lon
New Year's Eve *Saint-Sylvestre* f
sun·seel·ves·trer
New Zealand *Nouvelle-Zélande* f
noo·vel·zay·lond
news *les nouvelles* lay noo·vel
newsagent *marchand* m *de journaux*
mar·shon der zhoor·no
newspaper *journal* m zhoor·nal
next (month, etc) *prochain(e)* m/f
pro·shun/pro·shen
night *nuit* f nwee
night out *soirée* f swa·ray
nightclub *boîte* f bwat
no vacancy *complet* kom·play
no *non* non
noisy *bruyant(e)* m/f brew·yon(t)
nonsmoking *non-fumeur* non·few·mer
north *nord* m nor

nose *nez* m nay
notebook *carnet* m kar-nay
nothing *rien* ryun
now *maintenant* mun-ter-non
number *numéro* m new-may-ro
nurse *infirmier/infirmière* m/f
un-feer-myay/un-feer-myair
nut *noix* f nwa

O

off (spoiled) *mauvais(e)* m/f mo-vay(z)
oil *huile* f weel
oil (petrol) *pétrole* m pay-trol
old *vieux/vieille* m/f vyer/vyay
on *sur* sewr
onion *oignon* m o-nyon
on time *à l'heure* a ler
one *un(e)* m/f un/ewn
one-way (ticket) *(billet) simple* (bee-yay)
sum-pler
open *ouvert(e)* m/f oo-vair(t)
open *ouvrir* oo-vreer
opening hours *heures f pl d'ouverture*
er doo-vair-tewr
optometrist *optométriste* m&f
op-to-may-treest
orange *orange* o-ronzh
other *autre* o-trer
our *notre* no-trer
outside *dehors* der-or
overnight *pendant la nuit*
pon-don la nwee
overseas *outre-mer* oo-trer-mair
oysters *huîtres* f pl wee-trer

P

pacifier (dummy) *tétine* f tay-teen
package *paquet* m pa-kay
packet (general) *paquet* m pa-kay
padlock *cadenas* m kad-na

pain *douleur* f doo-ler
painful *douloureux/douloureuse* m/f
doo-loo-rer/doo-loo-rerz
painkiller *analgésique* m a-nal-zhay-zeek
painter *peintre* m pun-trer
painting (a work) *tableau* m ta-blo
painting (the art) *peinture* f pun-tewr
palace *palais* m pa-lay
pants *pantalon* m pon-ta-lon
panty liners *protège-slips* m pl
pro-tezh-sleep
pantyhose *collant* m ko-lon
paper *papier* m pa-pyay
paperwork *paperasserie* f pa-pras-ree
parcel *colis* m ko-lee
parents *parents* m pl pa-ron
park *parc* m park
park (a car) *garer (une voiture)* ga-ray
(ewn vwa-tewr)
party (night out) *soirée* f swa-ray
passenger *voyageur/voyageuse* m/f
vwa-ya-zher/vwa-ya-zherz
passport *passeport* m pas-por
passport number *numéro m de passeport*
new-may-ro der pas-por
path *chemin* m shmun
payment *paiement* m pay-mon
peach *pêche* f pesh
pear *poire* f pwar
pen (ballpoint) *stylo* m stee-lo
pencil *crayon* m kray-yon
penis *pénis* m pay-nees
penknife *canif* m ka-neef
pensioner *retraité(e)* m/f rer-tray-tay
pepper (bell) *poivron* m pwa-vron
perfume *parfum* m par-fum
petrol *essence* f ay-sons
petrol station *station-service* f
sta-syon-sair-vees
pharmacy *pharmacie* f far-ma-see
phone book *annuaire* m an-wair
phone box *cabine f téléphonique* ka-been
tay-lay-fo-neek

phone card *télécarte* f tay·lay·kart

photo *photo* f fo·to

photograph *prendre en photo* pron·drer on fo·to

photographer *photographe* m/f fo·to·graf

photography *photographie* f fo·to·gra·fee

phrasebook *recueil* m *d'expressions* rer·ker·yer dek·spray·syon

picnic *pique-nique* m peek·neek

pill *pilule* f pee·lewl

pillow *oreiller* m o·ray·yay

pillowcase *taie* f *d'oreiller* tay do·ray·yay

plane *avion* m a·vyon

plate *assiette* f a·syet

platform *quai* m kay

play (theatre) *pièce* f *de théâtre* pyes der tay·a·trer

plug (bath) *bonde* f bond

plug (electricity) *prise* f preez

plum *prune* f • *mirabelle* f prewn • mee·ra·bel

point *indiquer* un·dee·kay

police *police* f po·lees

police officer (in city) *policier* m po·lee·syay

police officer (in country) *gendarme* m zhon·darm

police station *commissariat* m ko·mee·sar·ya

pool (swimming) *piscine* f pee·seen

pork *porc* m por

postcode *code* m *postal* kod pos·tal

post office *bureau* m *de poste* bew·ro der post

postcard *carte postale* f kart pos·tal

potato *pomme* f *de terre* pom der tair

pound (money, weight) *livre* f leev·rer

prawns *crevettes* f pl roses kre·vet roz

pregnant *enceinte* on·sunt

prescription *ordonnance* f or·do·nons

present (gift) *cadeau* m ka·do

price *prix* m pree

printer (computer) *imprimante* f um·pree·mont

private *privé(e)* m/f pree·vay

prostitute *prostituée* f pro·stee·tway

pub (bar) *bar* m bar

public telephone *téléphone* m *public* tay·lay·fon per pewb·leek

public toilet *toilettes* f pl twa·let

purse *porte-monnaie* m port·mo·nay

Q

quiet *tranquille* trong·keel

R

radio *radio* f ra·dyo

railway station *gare* f gar

rain *pluie* f plwee

raincoat *imperméable* m um·pair·may·abler

rare *rare* rar

raspberry *framboise* f from·bwaz

rave *rave* f raiv

razor *rasoir* m ra·zwar

razor blade *lame* f *de rasoir* lam der ra·zwar

rear (seat etc) *arrière* a·ryair

receipt *reçu* m rer·sew

recommend *recommander* rer·ko·mon·day

refrigerator *réfrigérateur* m ray·free·zhay·ra·ter

refund *remboursement* m rom·boor·ser·mon

registered mail/post (by) *en recommandé* on rer·ko·mon·day

remote control *télécommande* f tay·lay·ko·mond

rent *louer* loo·ay

repair *réparer* ray·pa·ray

reservation *réservation* f ray·zair·va·syon

restaurant *restaurant* m res·to·ron
return (come back) *revenir* rerv·neer
return (ticket) *aller retour* m a·lay rer·toor
right (direction) *à droite* a drwat
ring (on finger) *bague* f bag
river *rivière* f ree·vyair
road *route* f root
romantic *romantique* ro·mon·teek
room *chambre* f shom·brer
room number *numéro* m *de chambre*
new·may·ro der shom·brer
ruins *ruines* f pl rween

S

safe *coffre-fort* m kof·rer·for
safe sex *rapports* m pl *sexuels protégés*
ra·por seks·wel pro·tay·zhay
sanitary napkin *serviette* f *hygiénique*
sair·vyet ee·zhay·neek
scarf *écharpe* f ay·sharp
science *science* f syons
scientist *scientifique* m/f syon·tee·feek
scissors *ciseaux* m pl see·zo
Scotland *Écosse* f ay·kos
sculpture *sculpture* f skewl·tewr
sea *mer* f mair
seafood *fruits* m pl *de mer* frwee der mair
season *saison* f say·zon
seat (place) *place* f plas
seatbelt *ceinture* f *de sécurité* sun·tewr
der say·kew·ree·tay
second class *de seconde classe*
der skond klas
self service *libre-service* m
lee·brer·sair·vees
service *service* m sair·vees
service charge *service* m sair·vees
service station *station-service* f
sta·syon·sair·vees
sex *sexe* m seks
shade *ombre* f om·brer

share (a dorm etc) *partager* par·ta·zhay
share (with) *partager (avec)* par·ta·zhay
(a·vek)
shave *se raser* ser ra·zay
shaving cream *mousse* f *à raser* moos
a ra·zay
sheet (bed) *drap* m dra
shirt *chemise* f sher·meez
shoe *chaussure* f sho·sewr
shoe shop *magasin* m *de chaussures*
ma·ga·zun der sho·sewr
shop *magasin* m ma·ga·zun
shop *faire des courses* fair day koors
shopping centre *centre* m *commercial*
son·trer ko·mair·syal
short (height) *court(e)* m/f koor(t)
shorts *short* m short
shoulder *épaule* f ay·pol
show *spectacle* m spek·ta·kler
show *montrer* mon·tray
shower *douche* f doosh
shrimps *crevettes* f pl *grises* kre·vet grees
shut *fermé(e)* m/f fair·may
sick *malade* ma·lad
silk *sole* f swa
silver *argent* m ar·zhon
single (person) *célibataire* say·lee·ba·tair
single room *chambre* f *pour une personne*
shom·brer poor ewn pair·son
sister *sœur* f ser
size (general) *taille* f tai
skiing *ski* m skee
skirt *jupe* f zhewp
sleep *dormir* dor·meer
sleeping bag *sac* m *de couchage* sak der
koo·shazh
sleeping car *wagon-lit* m va·gon·lee
slice *tranche* f tronsh
slide (film) *diapositive* f dya·po·zee·teev
slowly *lentement* lon·ter·mon
small *petit(e)* m/f per·tee/per·teet
smaller *plus petit(e)* m/f plew per·tee/·teet

smallest *le plus petit/la plus petite* m/f
ler plew per·tee/la plew per·teet

smell *odeur* f o·der

smoke *fumer* few·may

snack *casse-croûte* m kas·kroot

snow *neige* f nezh

soap *savon* m sa·von

socks *chaussettes* f sho·set

some *du/de la/des* m/f/pl dew/der la/day

son *fils* m fees

soon *bientôt* byun·to

south *sud* m sewd

souvenir *souvenir* m soov·neer

souvenir shop *magasin* m *de souvenirs*
ma·ga·zun der soov·neer

Spain *Espagne* f es·pa·nyer

speak *parler* par·lay

speed limit *limitation* f *de vitesse*
lee·mee·ta·syon der vee·tes

spinach *épinards* m pl ay·pee·nar

spoon *cuillère* f kwee·yair

sports store/shop *magasin* m *de sports*
ma·ga·zun der spor

sprain *entorse* f on·tors

spring (season) *printemps* m prun·tom

square (town) *place* f plas

stairway *escalier* m es·ka·lyay

stamp *timbre* m tum·brer

stand-by ticket *billet* m *stand-by* bee·yay
stond·bai

station *gare* f gar

stationer's (shop) *papeterie* f pa·pet·ree

stockings *bas* m ba

stolen *volé(e)* m/f vo·lay

stomach *estomac* m es·to·ma

stomachache (to have a) *avoir mal au*
ventre a·vwar mal o von·trer

Stop! *Arrêtez!* a·ray·tay

strawberry *fraise* f frez

street *rue* f rew

street market *braderie* f bra·dree

strike *grève* f grev

stroller *poussette* f poo·set

student *étudiant(e)* m/f ay·tew·dyon(t)

subtitles *sous-titres* m pl soo·tee·trer

subway *métro* m may·tro

suitcase *valise* f va·leez

summer *été* m ay·tay

sun *soleil* m so·lay

sunblock *écran* m *solaire total* ay·kron
so·lair to·tal

sunburn *coup* m *de soleil* koo der so·lay

sunglasses *lunettes* f *de soleil* lew·net
der so·lay

sunrise *lever* m *du soleil* ler·vay dew
so·lay

sunset *coucher* m *du soleil* koo·shay
dew so·lay

supermarket *supermarché* m
sew·pair·mar·shay

surface mail (land) *voie* f *de terre* vwa
der tair

surface mail (sea) *voie* f *maritime* vwa
ma·ree·teem

surname *nom* m *de famille* nom der
fa·mee·yer

sweater *pull* m pewl

sweet *sucré(e)* m/f sew·kray

swim *nager* na·zhay

swimming pool *piscine* f pee·seen

swimsuit *maillot* m *de bain* ma·yo der bun

T

tailor *tailleur* m ta·yer

tampon *tampon* m *hygiénique* tom·pon
ee·zhyay·neek

tanning lotion *crème* f *de bronzage* krem
der bron·zazh

tap *robinet* m ro·bee·nay

tasty *délicieux/délicieuse* m/f day·lees·yer/
day·lees·yerz

taxi *taxi* m tak·see

taxi stand *station f de taxi* sta·syon der tak·see

teacher *professeur* m pro·fay·ser

teaspoon *petite cuillère* f per·teet kwee·yair

telegram *télégramme* m tay·lay·gram

telephone *téléphone* m tay·lay·fon

telephone *téléphoner* tay·lay·fo·nay

telephone box *cabine f téléphonique* ka·been tay·lay·fo·neek

television *télé(vision) f* tay·lay(vee·zyon)

temperature *température* f tom·pay·ra·tewr

tennis *tennis* m tay·nees

tennis court *court m de tennis* koor der tay·nees

thank you *merci* mair·see

that (one) *cela* ser·la

theatre *théâtre* m tay·a·trer

there *là* la

thirsty (to be) *avoir soif* a·vwar swaf

this (one) *ceci* ser·see

throat *gorge* f gorzh

ticket *billet* m bee·yay

ticket machine *distributeur m de tickets* dee·stree·bew·ter der tee·kay

ticket office *guichet* m gee·shay

time *temps* m tom

time difference *décalage* m *horaire* day·ka·lazh o·rair

timetable *horaire* m o·rair

tin (can) *boîte* f bwat

tin opener *ouvre-boîte* m oo·vrer·bwat

tip (gratuity) *pourboire* m poor·bwar

tire *pneu* m pner

tired *fatigué(e)* m/f fa·tee·gay

tissues *mouchoirs* m *en papier* moo·shwar om pa·pyay

to *à* a

toast *pain grillé* m pun gree·yay

toaster *grille-pain* m greey·pun

today *aujourd'hui* o·zhoor·dwee

together *ensemble* on·som·bler

toilet *(toilettes f pl)* twa·let

toilet paper *papier m hygiénique* pa·pyay ee·zhyay·neek

tomato *tomate* f to·mat

tomorrow *demain* der·mun

tomorrow afternoon *demain après-midi* der·mun a·pray·mee·dee

tomorrow evening *demain soir* der·mun swar

tomorrow morning *demain matin* der·mun ma·tun

tonight *ce soir* ser swar

too (expensive etc) *trop* tro

toothache *mal m de dents* mal der don

toothbrush *brosse f à dents* bros a don

toothpaste *dentifrice* m don·tee·frees

torch (flashlight) *lampe f de poche* lomp der posh

tour *voyage* m vwa·yazh

tourist office *office de tourisme* m o·fees·der too·rees·mer

towel *serviette* f sair·vyet

train *train* m trun

train station *gare* f gar

transit lounge *salle f de transit* sal der tron·zeet

translate *traduire* tra·dweer

travel agency *agence f de voyage* a·zhons der vwa·yazh

travel sickness *mal m des transports* mal day trons·por

travellers cheque *chèque m de voyage* shek der vwa·yazh

trolley *chariot* m shar·yo

trousers *pantalon* m pon·ta·lon

try *essayer* ay·say·yay

T-shirt *t-shirt* m tee·shert

TV *télé* f tay·lay

tweezers *pince f à épiler* puns a ay·pee·lay

twin beds *lits* m pl *jumeaux* lee zhew·mo

two *deux* der

tyre *pneu* m pner

U English–French dictionary

LOOK UP

U

umbrella *parapluie* m pa·ra·plwee
uncomfortable *inconfortable*
ung·kon·for·ta·bler
underwear *sous-vêtements* m
soo·vet·mon
university *université* f
ew·nee·vair·see·tay
until (eg, Friday) *jusqu'à* zhew·ska
up *en haut* on o
urgent *urgent(e)* m/f ewr·zhon(t)
USA *les États Unis* m pl lay zay·taz ew·nee

V

vacancy *chambre* f *libre* shom·brer
lee·brer
vacant *libre* lee·brer
vacation *vacances* f pl va·kons
vaccination *vaccination* f vak·see·na·syon
validate *valider* va·lee·day
valuable *de valeur* der va·ler
veal *veau* m vo
vegetable *légume* m lay·gewm
vegetarian *végétarien/végétarienne* m/f
vay·zhay·ta·ryun/vay·zhay·ta·ryen
video recorder *magnétoscope* m
ma·nyay·to·skop
video tape *bande* f *vidéo* bond vee·day·o
view *vue* f vew
visa *visa* m vee·za

W

wait (for) *attendre* a·ton·drer
waiter *serveur/serveuse* m/f
sair·ver/sair·verz
waiting room *salle* f *d'attente* sal da·tont
wake (someone) up *réveiller* ray·vay·yay
Wales *Pays de Galle* m pay der gal
walk *marcher* mar·shay

warm *chaud(e)* m/f sho(d)
wash (something) *laver* la·vay
washing machine *machine* f *à laver*
ma·sheen a la·vay
watch *montre* f mon·trer
water *eau* f o
water bottle (hot) *bouillotte* f boo·yot
week *semaine* f ser·men
weekend *week-end* m week·end
west *ouest* m west
wheelchair *fauteuil* m *roulant* fo·ter·yee
roo·lon
when *quand* kon
where *où* oo
which *quel(le)* m/f kel
white *blanc/blanche* m/f blong/blonsh
who *qui* kee
why *pourquoi* poor·kwa
wife *femme* f fam
window *fenêtre* f fer·nay·trer
wine *vin* m vun
winter *hiver* m ee·vair
without *sans* son
woman *femme* f fam
wool *laine* f len
write *écrire* ay·kreer

Y

year *année* m a·nay
yes *oui* wee
yesterday *hier* ee·yair
you sg pol & pl *vous* voo
you inf *tu* tew
youth hostel *auberge* f *de jeunesse*
o·bairzh der zher·nes

Z

zip/zipper *fermeture* f *éclair* fair·mer·tewr
ay·klair
zoo *zoo* m zo

92

Nouns in this dictionary have their gender indicated by m (masculine) or f (feminine).
If it's a plural noun, you'll also see pl.
Where no gender is marked the word is either an adjective or a verb, with adjectives first.

A

auto m o-to *car*
à a *at*
acheter ash-tay *buy*
addition f a-dee-syon *bill (restaurant)* • *check (bill)*
aéroport m a-ay-ro-por *airport*
affaires f pl a-fair *business*
agence de voyage f a-zhons der vwa-yazh *travel agency*
agence immobilière f a-zhons ee-mo-bee-lyair *estate agency*
aider ay-day *help*
alcool m al-kol *alcohol*
aller a-lay *go*
aller retour m a-lay rer-toor *return (ticket)*
ambassade f om-ba-sad *embassy*
amende f a-mond *fine (penalty)*
ami(e) m/f a-mee *friend*
anglais(e) m/f ong-glay(z) *English*
année f a-nay *year*
anniversaire m a-nee-vair-sair *birthday*
annuaire m an-wair *phone book*
annuler a-new-lay *cancel*
antiquité f on-tee-kee-tay *antique*
appareil photo m a-pa-ray fo-to *camera*
appeler a-per-lay *call*
après-demain a-pray-der-mun *day after tomorrow (the)*
après midi m a-pray-mee-dee *afternoon*
argent m ar-zhon *money* • *silver*
arrêt d'autobus a-ray do-to-bews *bus stop*
arrivées f pl a-ree-vay *arrivals*
artisanat m ar-tee-za-na *crafts*
ascenseur m a-son-ser *lift* • *elevator*

assez a-say *enough*
assurance f a-sew-rons *insurance*
Attention! a-ton-syon *Careful!*
auberge de jeunesse f o-bairzh der zher-nes *youth hostel*
aujourd'hui o-zhoor-dwee *today*
automne m o-ton *fall (autumn)*
autoroute f o-to-root *highway* • *motorway (tollway)*
avant-hier a-von-tyair *day before yesterday (the)*
avion m a-vyon *aeroplane*

B

bac m bak *ferry*
bagages m pl ba-gazh *luggage*
baignoire f he-nywar *bath*
banque f bonk *bank*
bateau m ba-to *boat*
bâtiment m ba-tee-mon *building*
beau/belle m/f bo/bel *beautiful*
bébé m bay-bay *baby*
bientôt byun-to *soon*
bière f byair *beer*
bijoux m pl bee-zhoo *jewellery*
billet m bee-yay *ticket*
— **simple** sum-pler *one-way (ticket)*
blan(che) m/f blon(sh) *white*
bleu(e) m/f bler *blue*
boire bwar *drink*
boisson f bwa-son *drink*
boîte f bwat *box* • *nightclub*
boucherie f boosh-ree *butcher's shop*
boulangerie f boo-lon-zhree *bakery*
bouteille f boo-tay *bottle*
briquet m bree-kay *cigarette lighter*
brun/brune m/f brun/brewn *brown*

bureau m bew·ro *office*
 — **de poste** der post *post office*
 — **des objets trouvés** day zob·zhay troo·vay *lost property office*
(auto)bus m (o·to)bews *bus (city)*

C

cabine f **téléphonique** ka·been tay·lay·fo·neek *phone box*
cadeau m ka·do *present (gift)*
café m ka·fay *coffee • café*
caissier/caissière m/f kay·syay/kay·syair *cashier*
campagne f kom·pa·nyer *countryside*
canif m ka·neef *penknife*
(auto)car m (o·to)kar *bus (intercity)*
carte f kart *menu • map (of country)*
 — **d'embarquement** dom·bar·ker·mon *boarding pass*
 — **d'identité** dee·don·tee·tay *identification card (ID)*
 — **de crédit** der kray·dee *credit card*
 — **grise** greez *car owner's title*
 — **postale** pos·tal *postcard*
cassé(e) m/f ka·say *broken*
casse-croûte m kas·kroot *snack*
ceinture f **de sécurité** sun·tewr der say·kew·ree·tay *seatbelt*
célibataire m say·lee·ba·tair *single (person)*
cendrier m son·dree·yay *ashtray*
centre m **commercial** son·trer ko·mair·syal *shopping centre*
centre-ville m son·trer·veel *city centre*
chambre f shom·brer *room*
 — **à coucher** a koo·shay *bedroom*
 — **libre** lee·brer *vacancy*
 — **pour deux personnes** poor der pair·son *double room*
 — **pour une personne** poor ewn pair·son *single room*

changer shon·zhay *change*
chaque shak *each • every*
chaud(e) m/f sho(d) *hot • warm*
chauffé(e) m/f sho·fay *heated*
chaussettes f sho·set *socks*
chaussure f sho·sewr *shoe*
chemin m shmun *path*
chemise f sher·meez *shirt*
chèque m shek *check (banking) • cheque*
 — **de voyage** der vwa·yazh *travellers cheque*
cher/chère m/f shair *expensive*
chien m shyun *dog*
cimetière m seem·tyair *cemetery*
cirque m seerk *circus*
classe f **affaires** klas a·fair *business class*
classe f **touriste** klas too·reest *economy class*
clé f klay *key*
climatisé(e) m/f kee·ma·tee·zay *air-conditioned*
code m **postal** kod pos·tal *post code*
coffre-fort m kof·rer·for *safe*
collant m ko·lon *pantyhose*
commissariat m ko·mee·sar·ya *police station*
complet kom·play *no vacancy*
complet/complète m/f kom·play/kom·plet *booked up*
compris(e) m/f kom·pree(z) *included*
compte m kont *account*
 — **bancaire** bong·kair *bank account*
confirmer kon·feer·may *confirm (a booking)*
confortable kon·for·ta·bler *comfortable*
consigne f kon·see·nyer *left luggage (office)*
 — **automatique** o·to·ma·teek *luggage lockers*
couche f koosh *nappy • diaper*
court(e) m/f koor(t) *short (height)*

couvert m koo-vair *cover charge*
couverture f koo-vair-tewr *blanket*
cuir m kweer *leather*
cuisine f kwee-zeen *kitchen*
cuisinier/cuisinière m/f kwee-zee-nyay/ kwee-zee-nyair *cook*
cybercafé m see-bair-ka-fay *Internet cafe*

D

date f **de naissance** dat der nay-sons *date of birth*
déjeuner m day-zher-nay *lunch*
demain der-mun *tomorrow*
— **après-midi** a-pray-mee-dee *tomorrow afternoon*
— **matin** ma-tun *tomorrow morning*
— **soir** swar *tomorrow evening*
départ m day-par *departure*
dépôt m day-po *deposit*
dernier/dernière m/f dalr-nyay/ dair-nyair *last (previous)*
diapositive f dya-po-zee-teev *slide (film)*
dictionnaire m deek-syo-nair *dictionary*
dîner m dee-nay *dinner*
direct(e) m/f dee-rekt *direct*
disquaire m dee-skair *music shop*
disque m deesk *disk (CD-ROM)*
disquette f dees-ket *disk (floppy)*
distributeur m **de tickets** dee-stree-bew-ter der tee-kay *ticket machine*
doigt m dwa *finger*
dos m do *back (body)*
douane f dwan *customs*
douche f doosh *shower*
draps m dra *bed linen*

E

eau f o *water*
— **minérale** mee-nay-ral *mineral water*

échange m ay-shonzh *exchange*
échanger ay-shon-zhay *change (money) • exchange*
église f ay-gleez *church*
en retard on rer-tar *late*
enfant m/f on-fon *child*
enregistrement on-rer-zhee-strer-mon *check-in (desk)*
ensemble on-som-bler *together*
entracte m on-trakt *intermission*
entrée f on-tray *entry*
entreprise f on-trer-preez *company*
enveloppe f on-vlop *envelope*
épicerie f ay-pee-sree *grocery*
escalier m es-ka-lyay *stairway*
essence f ay-sons *gasoline • petrol*
est m est *east*
étage m ay-tazh *floor (storey)*
été m ay-tay *summer*
étranger/étrangère m/f ay tron zhay/ ay-tron-zhair *foreign*
étudiant(e) m/f ay-tew-dyon(t) *student*
excédent ek-say-don *excess (baggage)*
exposition f ek-spo-zee-syon *exhibition*
(par) exprès eks-pres *express (mail)*

F

faire les courses fair lay koors *go shopping*
famille f fa-mee-yer *family*
félicitations fay-lee-see-ta-syon *congratulations*
femme f fam *wife • woman*
fenêtre f fer-nay-trer *window*
fermé(e) m/f fair-may *closed*
— **à clé** m/t a klay *locked*
fièvre f fyev-rer *fever*
fille f fee-yer *daughter • girl*
fils m fees *son*
forêt f fo-ray *forest*
frais/fraîche m/f fray/fresh *fresh*

franchise f fron·sheez *baggage allowance*
freins m *frun brakes*
frère m *frair brother*
froid(e) m/f frwa(d) *cold*
frontière f fron·tyair *border*
fumer few·may *smoke*

G

gants m pl gon *gloves*
garçon m gar·son *boy*
gare f gar *train station*
— **routière** roo·tyair *bus station*
gaz m gaz *gas (for cooking)*
gendarme m zhon·darm *police officer (in country)*
gentil(le) m/f zhon·tee *kind (nice)*
grand(e) m/f gron(d) *big*
grand lit m gron lee *double bed*
grand magasin m gron ma·ga·zun *department store*
gratuit(e) m/f gra·twee(t) *free (gratis)*
grippe f greep *flu*
gris(e) m/f gree(z) *grey*
groupe m *sanguin* groop song·gun *blood group*
guichet m gee·shay *ticket office*
— **automatique de banque (GAB)** o·to·ma·teek der bonk *automatic teller machine (ATM)*

H

heure f er *hour*
heures f pl **d'ouverture** er doo·vair·tewr *opening hours*
hier ee·yair *yesterday*
hiver m ee·vair *winter*
homme m om *man*
hôpital m o·pee·tal *hospital*
horaire m o·rair *timetable*
hors service or sair·vees *out of order*
hôtel m o·tel *hotel*
huile f weel *oil*

I

ici ee·see *here*
immatriculation ee·ma·tree·kew·la·syon *car registration*
interprète m/f un·tair·pret *interpreter*
itinéraire m ee·tee·nay·rair *itinerary*
ivre ee·vrer *drunk*

J

jardin m zhar·dun *garden*
jean m zheen *jeans*
jour m zhoor *day*
journal m zhoor·nal *newspaper*
jupe f zhewp *skirt*

L

laine f len *wool*
lait m lay *milk*
laver la·vay *wash (something)*
laverie f lav·ree *launderette*
légume m lay·gewm *vegetable*
lettre f lay·trer *letter*
librairie f lee·bray·ree *bookshop*
libre m/f lee·brer *vacant*
libre-service m lee·brer·sair·vees *self service*
lin m lun *linen (material)*
linge m lunzh *laundry (clothes)*
lit m lee *bed*
lits m pl **jumeaux** lee zhew·mo *twin beds*
livre m leev·rer *book*
livre f leev·rer *pound (money, weight)*
location f **de voitures** lo·ka·syon der vwa·tewr *car hire*
logement m lozh·mon *accommodation*
louer loo·ay *hire • rent*
lune f **de miel** lewn der myel *honeymoon*
lunettes f pl lew·net *glasses (spectacles)*

M

machine f **à laver** ma·sheen a la·vay
    washing machine
magasin m ma·ga·zun *shop*
magnétoscope m ma·nyay·to·skop *video
    recorder*
maintenant mun·ter·non *now*
malade ma·lad *sick*
manger mon·zhay *eat*
manteau m mon·to *coat*
maquillage m ma·kee·yazh *make-up*
marchand m **de journaux** mar·shon der
    zhoor·no *newsagent*
marché m mar·shay *market*
    — **aux puces** o pews *fleamarket*
marcher mar·shay *walk*
mari m ma·ree *husband*
matin m ma·tun *morning*
mauvais(e) m/f mo·vay(z) *bad*
médecin m mayd·sun *doctor*
médicament m may·dee·ka·mon
    medicine (medication)
mer f mair *sea*
mère f mair *mother*
midi m mee·dee *midday • noon*
minuit f mee·nwee *midnight*
mode f mod *fashion*
modem m mo·dem *modem*
mois m mwa *month*
moitié f mwa·tyay *half*
monnaie f mo·nay *change (coins)*
montagne f mon·ta·nyer *mountain*
montre f mon·trer *watch*
moto f mo·to *motorcycle*
musée m mew·zay *art gallery • museum*

N

nager na·zhay *swim*
neige f nezh *snow*
nettoyage m net·wa·yazh *cleaning*
nettoyer net·wa·yay *clean*
Noël m no·el *Christmas*

noir et blanc nwar ay blong *B&W (film)*
noir(e) m/f nwar *black*
nom m nom *name*
    — **de famille** der fa·mee·yer *surname*
non-fumeur non·few·mer *nonsmoking*
nord m nor *north*
nuit f nwee *night*
numéro m new·may·ro *number*
    — **de chambre** der shom·brer *room
    number*
    — **de passeport** der pas·por *passport
    number*

O

occupé(e) m/f o·kew·pay *busy*
office de tourisme m o·fees·der
    too·rees·mer *tourist office*
or m or *gold*
orange f o·ronzh *orange*
ordinateur m or·dee·na·ter *computer*
    — **portable** por·ta·bler *laptop*
ordonnance f or·do·nons *prescription*
oreiller m o·ray·yay *pillow*
où oo *where*
ouest m west *west*
ouvert(e) m/f oo·vair(t) *open*

P

pain m pun *bread*
palais m pa·lay *palace*
pantalon m pon·ta·lon *pants • trousers*
papeterie f pa·pet·ree *stationer's (shop)*
papier m pa·pyay *paper*
partager par·ta·zhay *share (a dorm etc)*
partir par·teer *depart (leave)*
passeport m pas·por *passport*
peintre m pun·trer *painter*
peinture f pun·tewr *painting (the art)*
pellicule f pay·lee·kewl *film (for camera)*
pension f pon·syon *boarding house*
    — **de famille** der fa·mee·yer
    guesthouse

perdu(e) m/f pair·dew *lost*
père m pair *father*
permis m de conduire pair·mee der kon·dweer *driver's licence*
petit ami m per·tee a·mee *boyfriend*
petit déjeuner m per·tee day·zher·nay *breakfast*
petite amie f per·teet a·mee *girlfriend*
pièce f d'identité pyes dee·don·tee·tay *identification*
pièce f de théâtre pyes der tay·a·trer *play (theatre)*
pièces f pl pyes *coins*
pile f peel *battery*
pique-nique m peek·neek *picnic*
piscine f pee·seen *swimming pool*
place f plas *seat (place)* • *square (town)*
plage f plazh *beach*
plan m plon *map (of town)*
plat m pla *dish*
plus tard plew·tar *later*
poissonnerie f pwa·son·ree *fish shop*
policier m po·lee·syay *police officer (in city)*
poste f post *mail (postal system)*
pourboire m poor·bwar *tip (gratuity)*
pourquoi poor·kwa *why*
première classe f prer·myair klas *first class*
prénom m pray·non *Christian name*
préservatif m pray·zair·va·teef *condom*
printemps m prun·tom *spring (season)*
prix m pree *price*
prochain(e) m/f pro·shun/pro·shen *next (month)*
pull m pewl *jumper (sweater)*

Q

quai m kay *platform*
quand kon *when*
quel(le) m/f kel *which*
qui kee *who*
quotidien(ne) m/f ko·tee·dyun/ko·tee·dyen *daily*

R

rapide ra·peed *fast*
rapport m ra·por *connection*
reconnaissant(e) m/f rer·ko·nay·son(t) *grateful*
reçu m rer·sew *receipt*
recueil m d'expressions rer·ker·yer dek·spray·syon *phrasebook*
remboursement m rom·boor·ser·mon *refund*
remise f rer·meez *discount*
rendez-vous m ron·day·voo *appointment*
renseignements m pl ron·sen·yer·mon *information*
réparer ray·pa·ray *repair*
repas m rer·pa *meal*
réserver ray·zair·vay *book (make a booking)*
retard m rer·tard *delay*
retrait m des bagages rer·tray day ba·gazh *baggage claim*
retraité(e) m/f rer·tray·tay *pensioner*
réveil m ray·vay *alarm clock*
revenir rerv·neer *return (come back)*
robe f rob *dress*
rose roz *pink*
rouge roozh *red*
route f root *road*
rue f rew *street*

S

sac m sak *bag*
— **à dos** a do *backpack*
— **de couchage** der koo·shazh *sleeping bag*
saison f say·zon *season*
sale sal *dirty*
salle f sal *room*
— **d'attente** da·tont *waiting room*
— **de bain** der bun *bathroom*
— **de transit** der tron·zeet *transit lounge*
salon m de beauté sa·lon der bo·tay *beauty salon*

sans son *without*
sec/sèche m/f sek/sesh *dry*
semaine f ser·men *week*
sentier m son·tyay *footpath*
service m sair·vees *service charge*
serviette f sair·vyet *briefcase • towel*
sœur f ser *sister*
soie f swa *silk*
soir m swar *evening*
soirée f swa·ray *party (night out)*
sortie f sor·tee *exit*
sortir sor·teer *go out*
sous-titres m soo·tee·trer *subtitles*
sous-vêtements m soo·vet·mon
   underwear
soutien-gorge m soo·tyung·gorzh *bra*
sparadrap m spa·ra·dra *Band-Aid*
spectacle m spek·ta·kler *show*
station f de métro sta·syon der may·tro
   metro station
station f de taxi sta·syon der tak·see
   taxi stand
station-service f sta·syon·sair·vees
   petrol station
sud m sewd *south*
supérette f de quartier sew·pay·ret der
   kar·tyay *convenience store*
supermarché m sew·pair·mar·shay
   supermarket

T

tableau m ta·blo *painting (a work)*
taie f d'oreiller tay do·ray·yay *pillowcase*
taille f tai *size (general)*
tailleur m ta·yer *tailor*
tante f tont *aunt*
tarif m ta·reef *fare*
taux m de change to der shonzh
   exchange rate
taxe f d'aéroport taks da·ay·ro·por
   airport tax
télécarte f tay·lay·kart *phone card*

téléphone m portable tay·lay·fon
   por·ta·bler *mobile phone*
télésiège m tay·lay·syezh *chairlift (skiing)*
timbre m tum·brer *stamp*
tôt to *early*
tout(e) m/f too(t) *everything*
traiteur m tre·ter *delicatessen*
toux f too *cough*

V

vacances f pl va·kons *holidays*
valider va·lee·day *validate*
valise f va·leez *suitcase*
vélo m vay·lo *bicycle*
vert(e) m/f vair(t) *green*
veste f vest *jacket*
vestiaire m vays·tyair *cloakroom*
vêtements m pl vet·mon *clothing*
viande f vyond *meat*
ville f veel *city*
vin m vun *wine*
visite f guidée vee·zeet gee·day *guided
   tour*
voie de terre vwa der tair *surface mail
   (land)*
voie maritime vwa ma·ree·teem *surface
   mail (sea)*
voiture f vwa·tewr *car*
vol m vol *flight*
volé(e) m/f vo·lay *stolen*
voyage m vwa·yazh *tour*
   — d'affaires da·fair *business trip*
voyageur/voyageuse m/f vwa·ya·zher/
   vwa·ya·zherz *passenger*
vue f vew *view*

W

wagon-lit m va·gon·lee *sleeping car*
wagon-restaurant m va·gon·res·to·ron
   dining car

A

abbreviations	12
accidents	68
accommodation	61
addresses	15
admission	22
age	18
air-conditioning (transport)	56
allergies	73
allergies (food)	39
appointments	67
Arc de Triomphe	25
arranging to meet	33
art	21
ATM	49

B

baggage	57
ballet	32
banking	49
bargaining	29
bars	32, 37
bed and breakfast accommodation	61
beer	37
beliefs	19
beverages (alcoholic)	37
beverages (nonalcoholic)	36
bill (restaurant)	36
bookings (accommodation)	62
bookings (restaurant)	34
bookings (transport)	55
bookshops	30
breakfast	34, 63
bus	57
business	66
business cards	66
business equipment	67
buying clothes & shoes	29
buying food	38
buying things	27

C

cafes	32
camping ground	61
car hire	59

cash advances

cash advances	50
CDs	31
cell phones	51
Centre Pompidou	25
Chartres	24
checking out (accommodation)	65
chemist	70
Cimetière du Père Lachaise	25
cinema	32, 33
citizenship	16
civilities	13
Claude Monet Museum	24
clothes	29
clubs	32
coffee	36
collect calls	51
colours	74
commissions	50
compass points	54
complaints (accommodation)	64
compliments (accommodation)	65
computers	52, 67
concerts	32
conditions (medical)	72
conferences	66
cooking methods	36
courses (food)	40
credit cards	28
crime	69

D

dates	76
days of the week	75
day trips (from Paris)	24
debit cards	28
departure times	54
developing photos	31
diets (special)	39
dining establishments	35
dining out	34, 35
dinner	34
directions	53
discounts	22
dishes	41
Disneyland Paris	24
doctor	70
drinking	34, 37

drinks.. 40
drinks (alcoholic)........................... 37
drinks (nonalcoholic).................... 36
drugs (medical).............................. 71
duration of stay............................. 15

E

eateries.. 34
eateries (box)................................. 35
eating... 34
eating out.............................. 34, 35
Eiffel Tower.................................... 26
email....................................... 52, 67
emergencies.................................... 68
emotions.. 18
entertainment................................ 32
entertainment guides............. 30, 32
essential language.......................... 13
events.. 32
exchange (currency)...................... 49
exchange rates................................ 50
exchanging goods........................... 28
excursions.. 22
exhibitions....................................... 21

F

family.. 14, 17
fares (taxi)....................................... 58
fares (transport)............................. 56
feelings.. 18
films... 33
film (photography)......................... 31
film guides....................................... 32
finding your way............................. 53
Fontainebleau.................................. 24
food allergies................................... 40
food shopping................................. 38
footwear... 29
French eateries................................ 35
French food...................................... 41

G

galleries.. 21
gas (petrol)...................................... 60
gay venues....................................... 32
getting around................................ 54

getting help..................................... 68
going out... 32
goodbyes.. 13
greetings.. 13
grocery shopping........................... 38
guidebooks...................................... 20
guided tours.................................... 22
guides (tourist).............................. 20

H

health... 70
health problems.............................. 72
hobbies... 33
hotels.. 61
hotel facilities................................. 63

I

illnesses.. 72
insurance (travel)............................ 70
interests... 33
internet cafes.................................. 52
interpreters..................................... 67
introductions.................................. 14
introductions (business)................ 66

J

Jardin du Luxembourg.................... 25
jobs... 17
juice.. 36

L

language difficulties........................ 15
lost luggage..................................... 57
lost possessions.............................. 69
luggage... 57
luggage lockers............................... 57
lunch... 34

M

mail... 49
maps... 20, 30
marital status.................................. 17
meals.. 34
medical conditions......................... 72
medication............................... 71, 73

meeting people 13
meeting up 33
menu items 41
menu terms 40
methods of payment 28, 63
metro 57
mobile phones 51
modes of transport 54
money 28, 49
months 75
Montmartre 25
motorbike hire 59
Musée d'Orsay 26
Musée de Claude Monet 24
Musée du Louvre 26
Musée Rodin 26
museums 21
music 30

N

names 14
nationalities 16
newspapers 30
nightclubs 32
non-smoking section (restaurant) 34
non-smoking section (transport) 56
Notre Dame 26
numbers 74

O

occupations 17
opening hours 21, 22
opera 32
optometrist 70
ordering a meal 36
ordering drinks 37

P

paying 28
personal details 16
petrol 60
pharmacy 70
phone numbers 15
photography 31
photos 21, 31
places of interest 20

places to stay 61
pleasantries 14
points of the compass 54
police 69
Pompidou Centre 25
post office 49
prescriptions 73
prices 28
problems (health) 72
problems (language) 15
public transport 57
pubs 32, 37
purchasing 28
purpose of travel 14

R

receipts 28
receipt (accommodation) 63
recommendations (accommodation) 61
recommendations (restaurants) 34
religion 19
requests (accommodation) 63
reservations (accommodation) 62
reservations (restaurant) 34
reservations (transport) 56
restaurants 32, 35
returning goods 28
reverse-charge calls 51
road signs 60

S

seasons 76
seating (transport) 55, 56
self-service restaurants 35
sending mail 49
sensations 18
shoes 29
shopping 27
shopping (food) 38
shopping precincts (Paris) 29
sicknesses 72
sightseeing 20
signs (road) 60
SIM cards 51
sizes (clothing & footwear) 30
small talk 13

snack.....................................34
socialising (business).....................67
soda.....................................36
soft drinks.....................................36
specialities (food).....................41
specialty shops.....................29
speed limit.....................................60
spirits.....................................37
stationary.....................................30
stolen possessions.....................69
study.....................................17
subjects (study).....................17
symptoms.....................................71

T

tarrifs (hotel).....................................62
tastes.....................................33
taxi.....................................57
taxi fares.....................................58
tea.....................................36
telling the time.....................75
theatre.....................................32
the Louvre.....................................26
tickets (transport).....................55
time.....................................75
titles.....................................13
toilets.....................................68
top 10 sights (Paris).....................25
tourist sights.....................20
tours.....................................22

Tour Eiffel.....................................26
train.....................................57
transport.....................................53
travellers cheques.....................28, 50
travel insurance.....................70

U

understanding.....................16

V

vaccinations.....................................71
vegan food.....................................39
vegetarian food.....................39
venues.....................................32
Versailles.....................................24

W

water.....................................37
weather.....................................19
weights.....................................38
wine.....................................37
withdrawals (money).....................50
work.....................................17

Y

youth hostels.....................61

he only word you know.

...oser and shout louder.

C. When the barman doesn't understand your order, you point frantically at the beer.

...eriences

...oducts ...

...nguage

...lish as it's spoken

around the world – learn and laugh

- **Lonely Planet Fast Talk & Fast Talk Audio** – essential phrases for short trips and